SUGAR SKULLS

GRAYSCALE COLORING BOOK FOR ADULTS

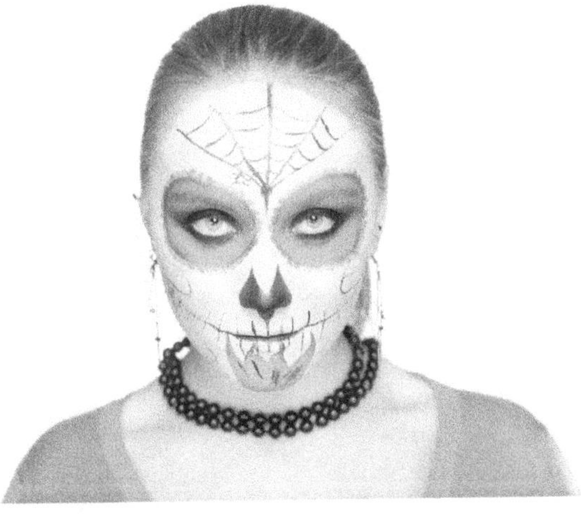

Majestic COLORING

www.MajesticColoring.com

ISBN: 978-1530527502

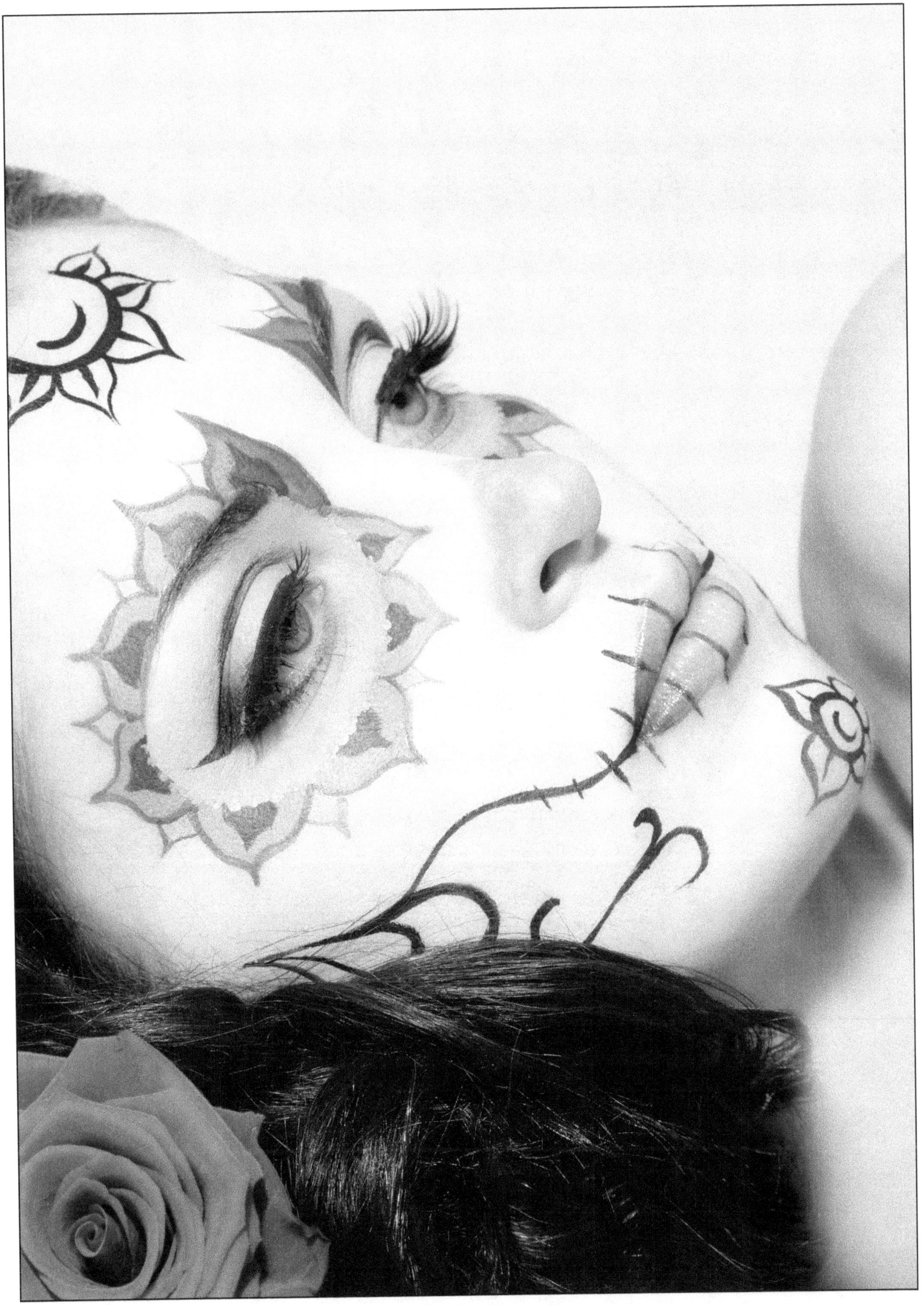

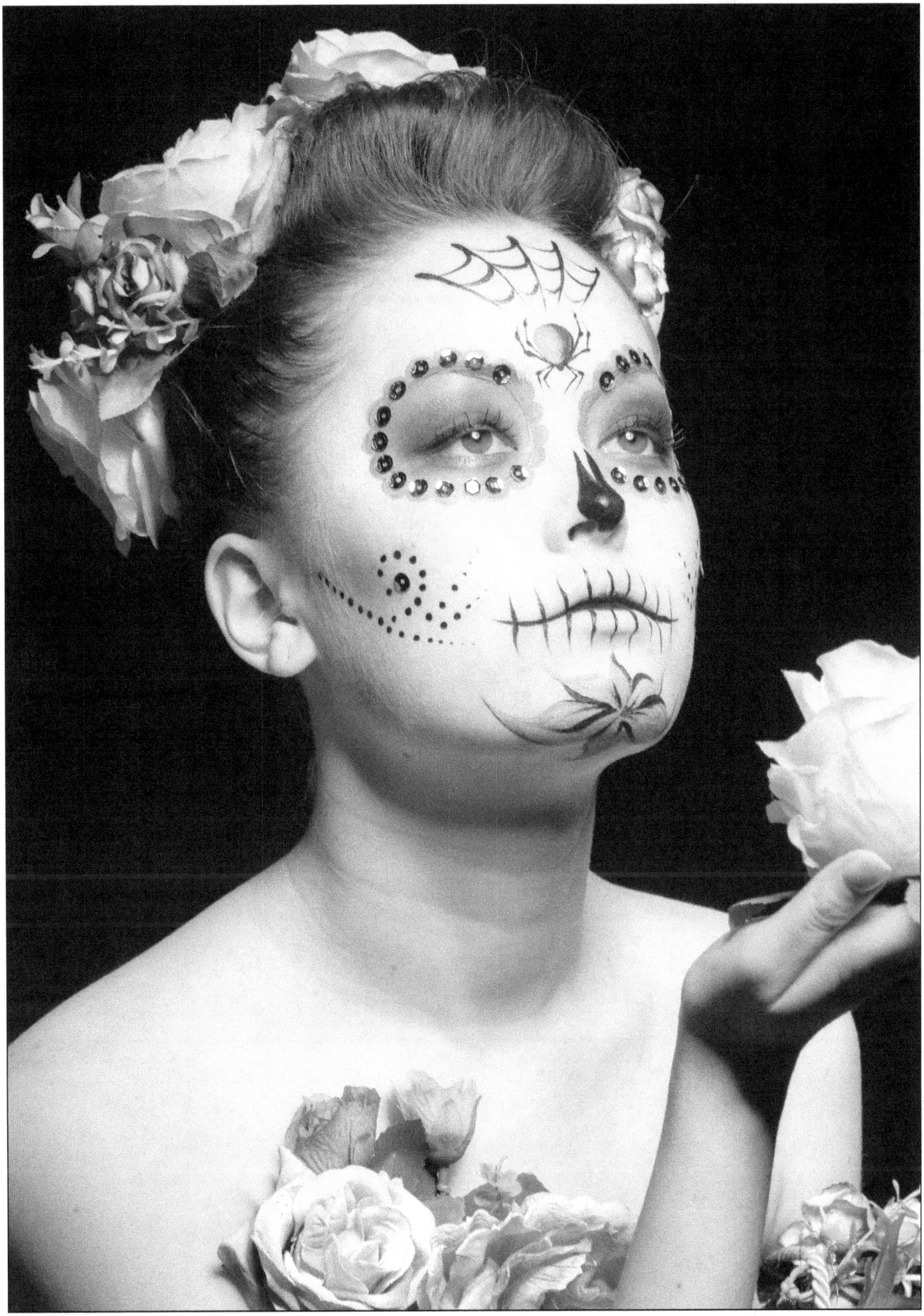

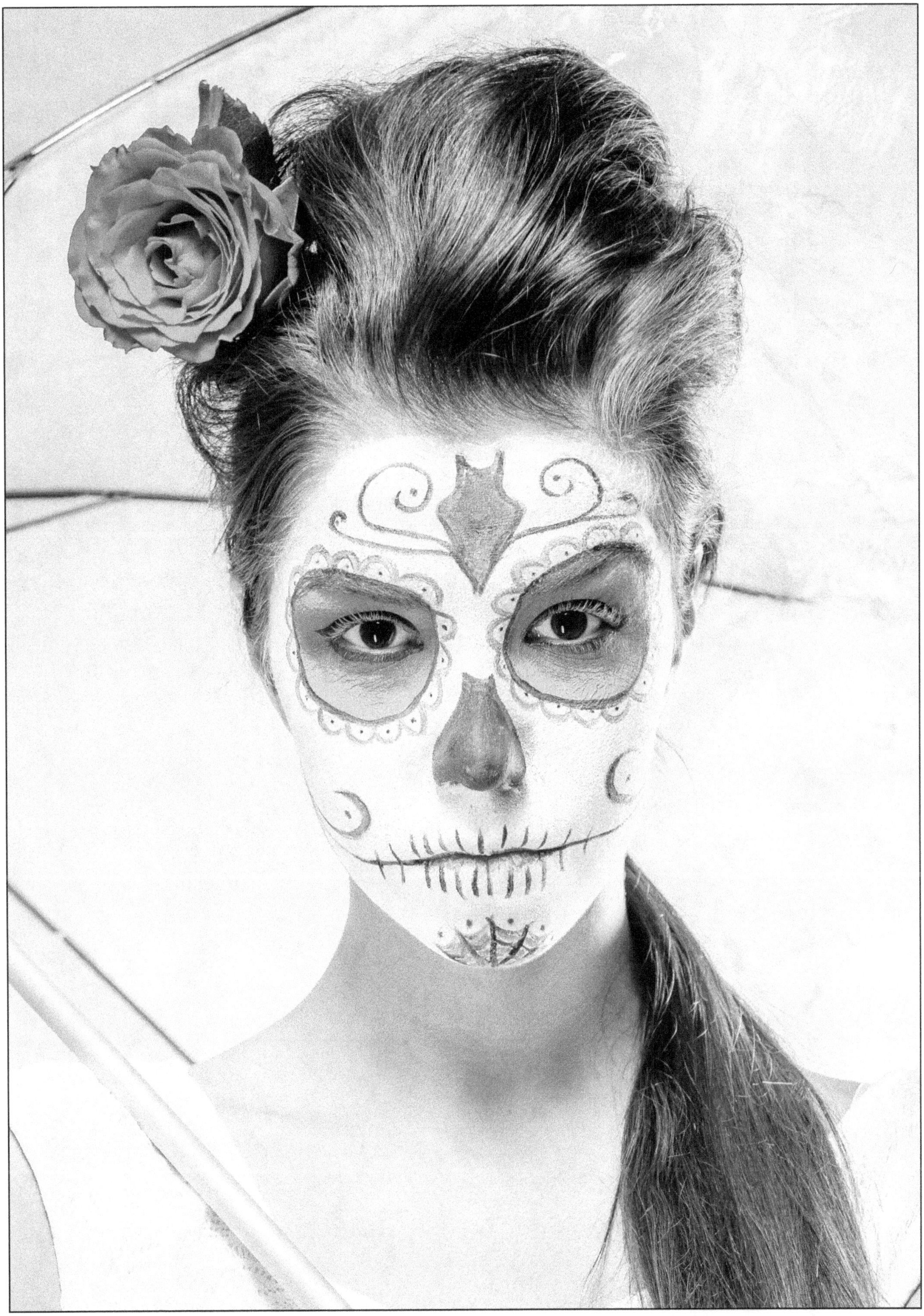

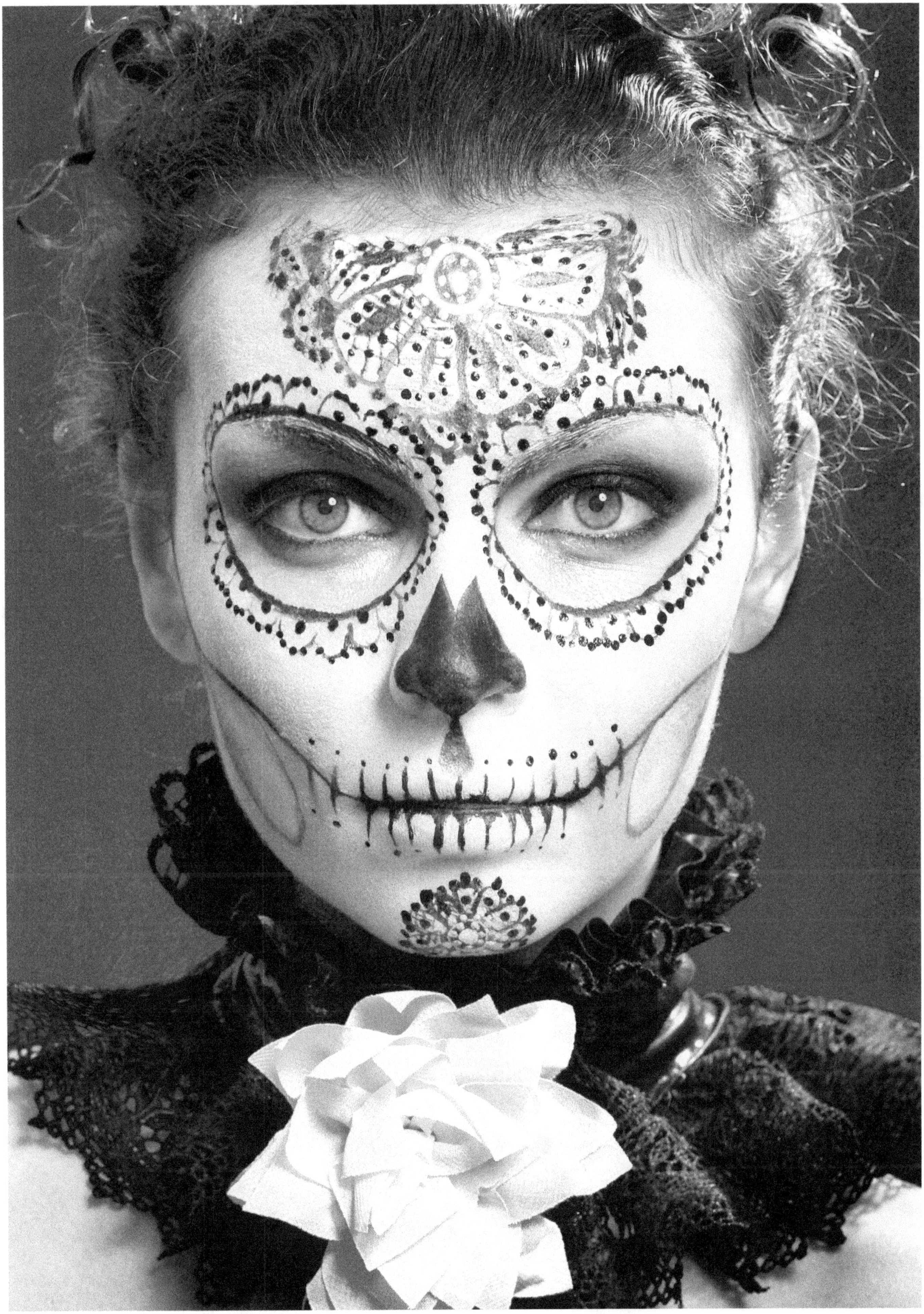

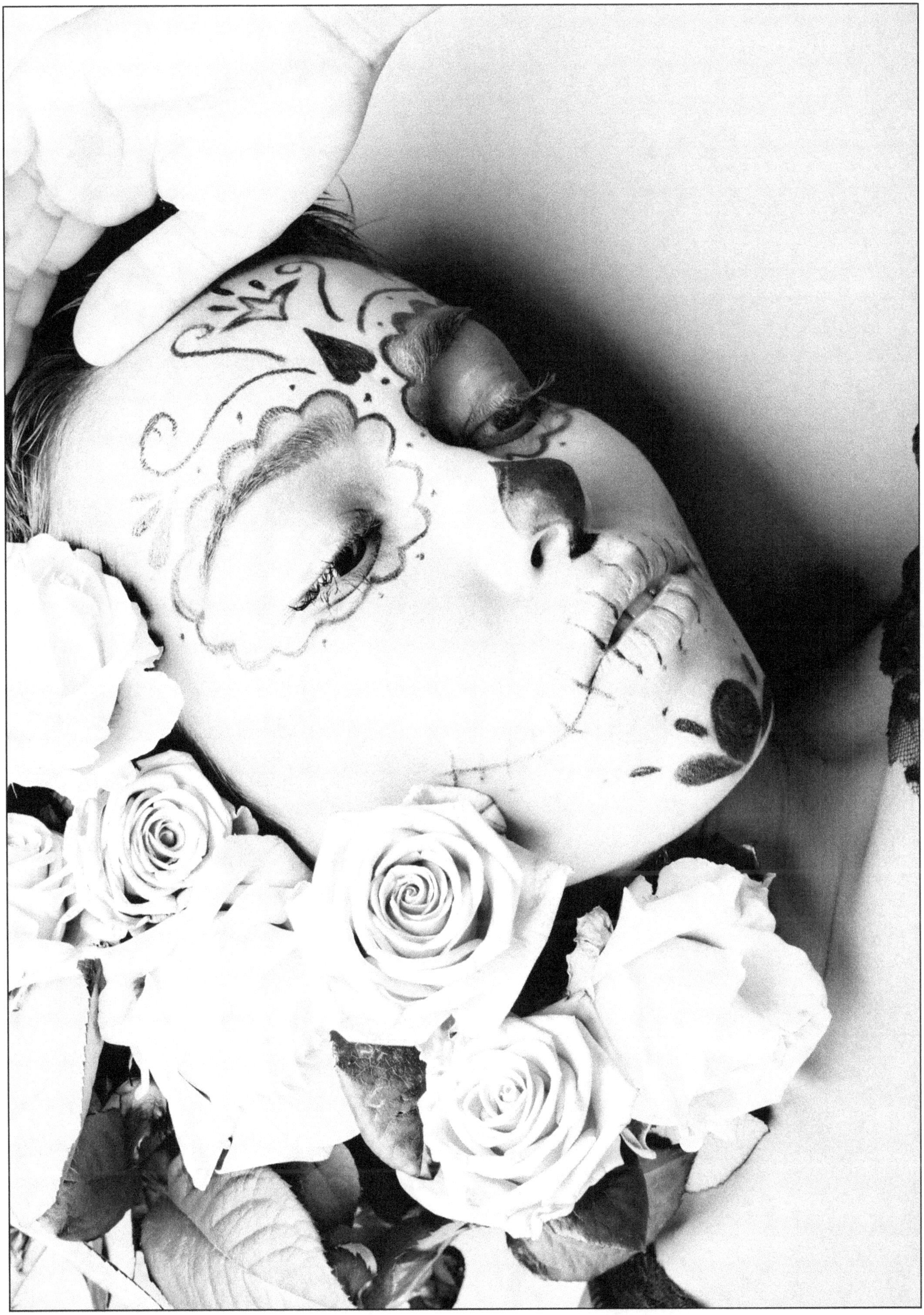

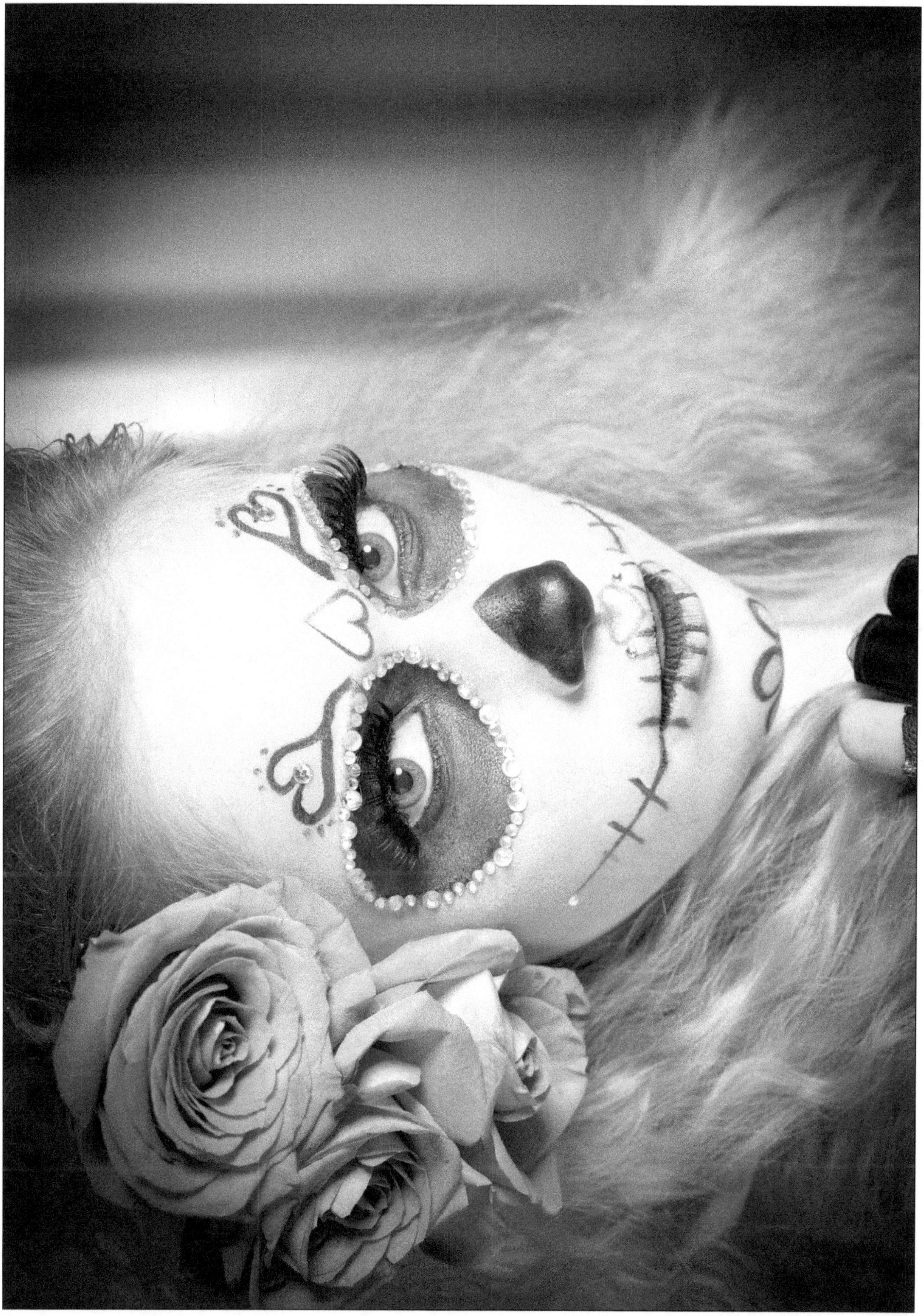

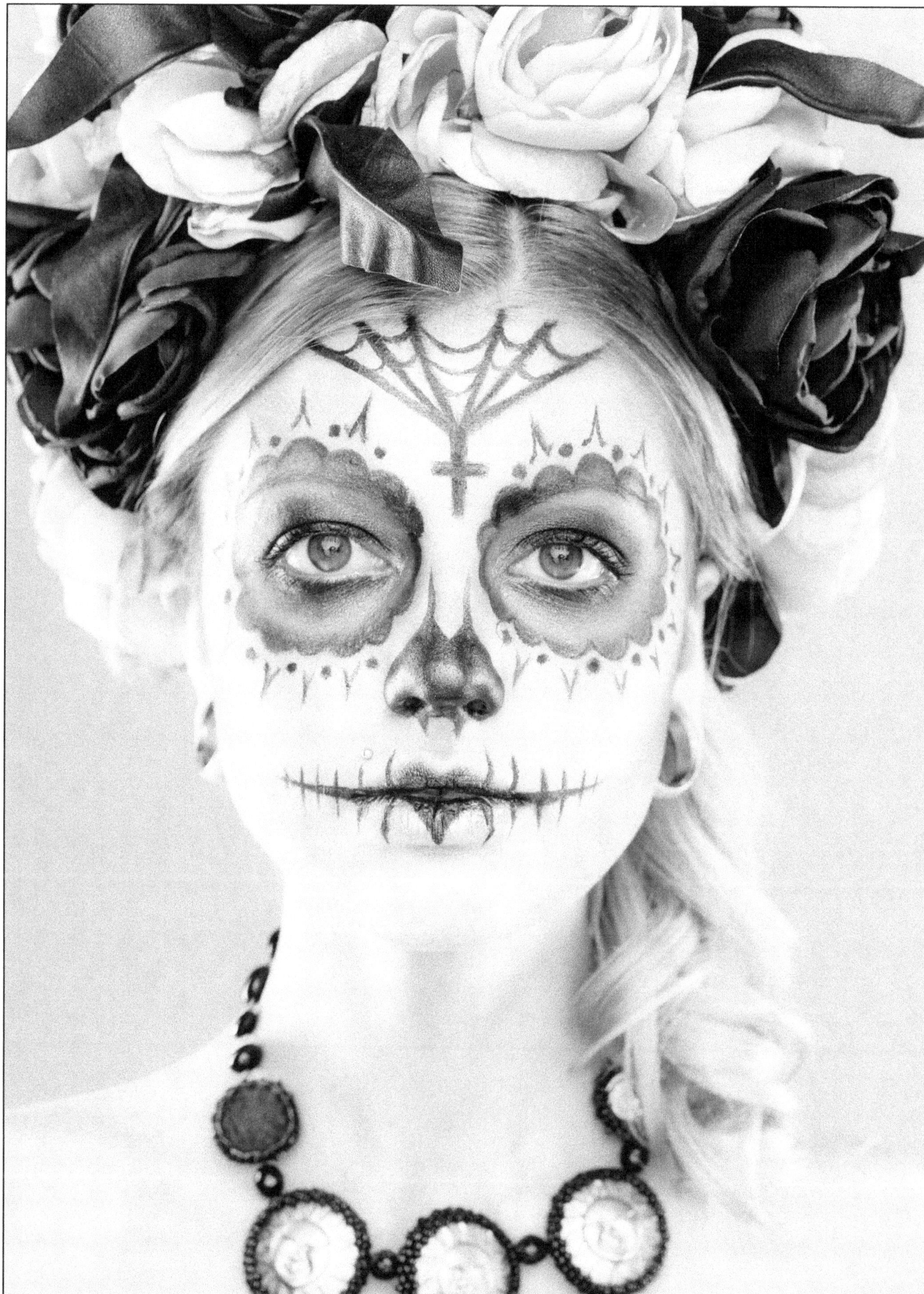

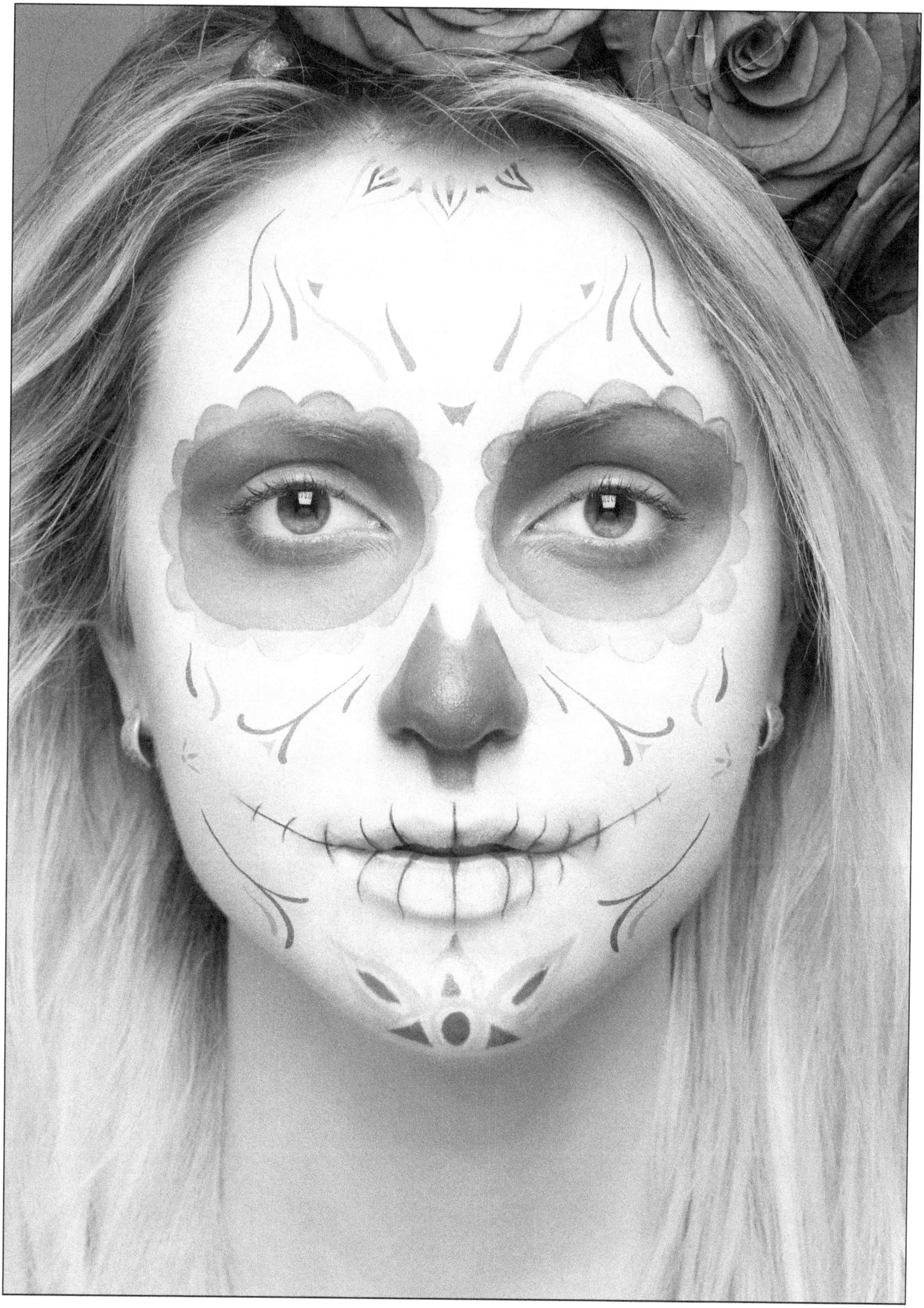

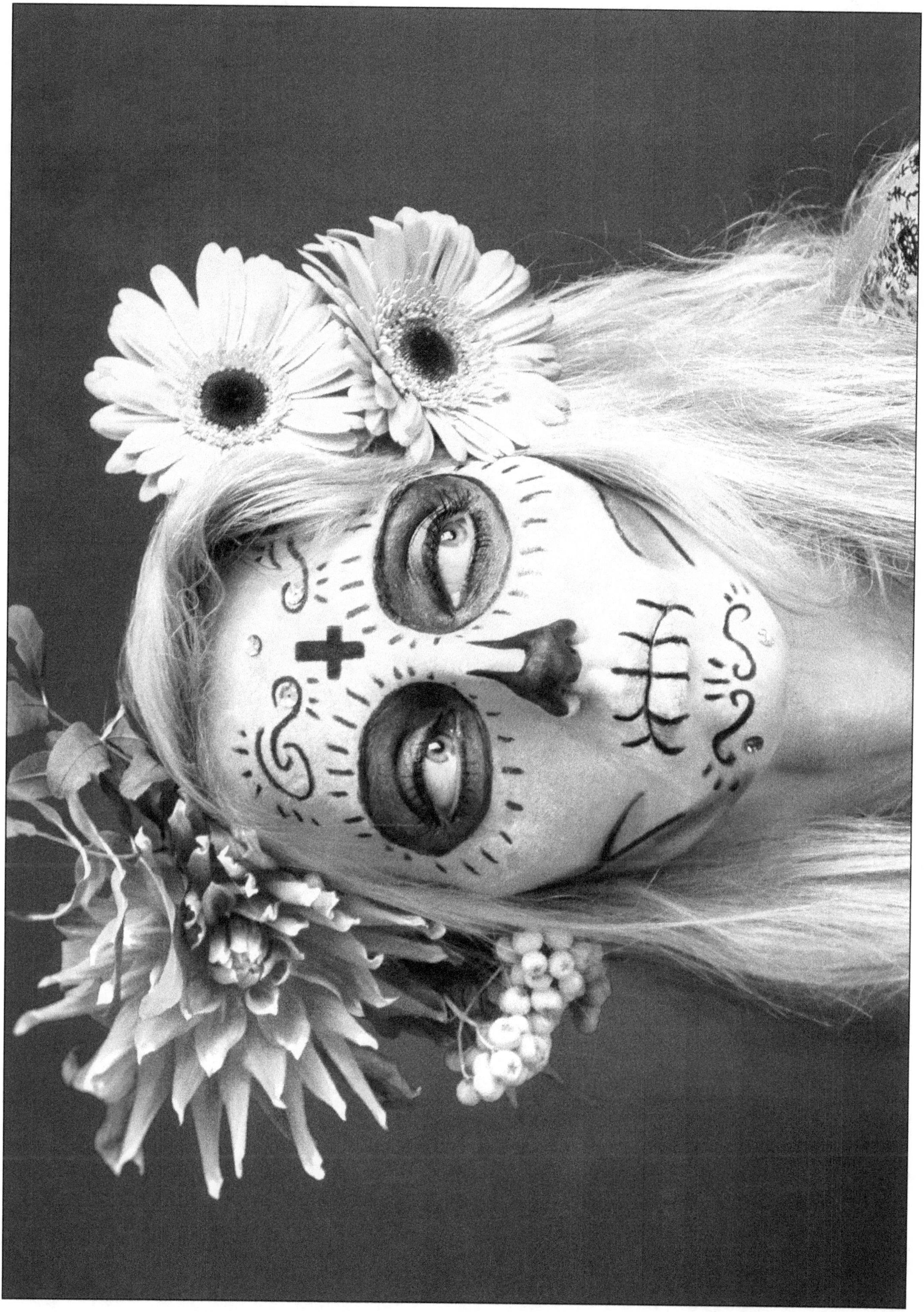

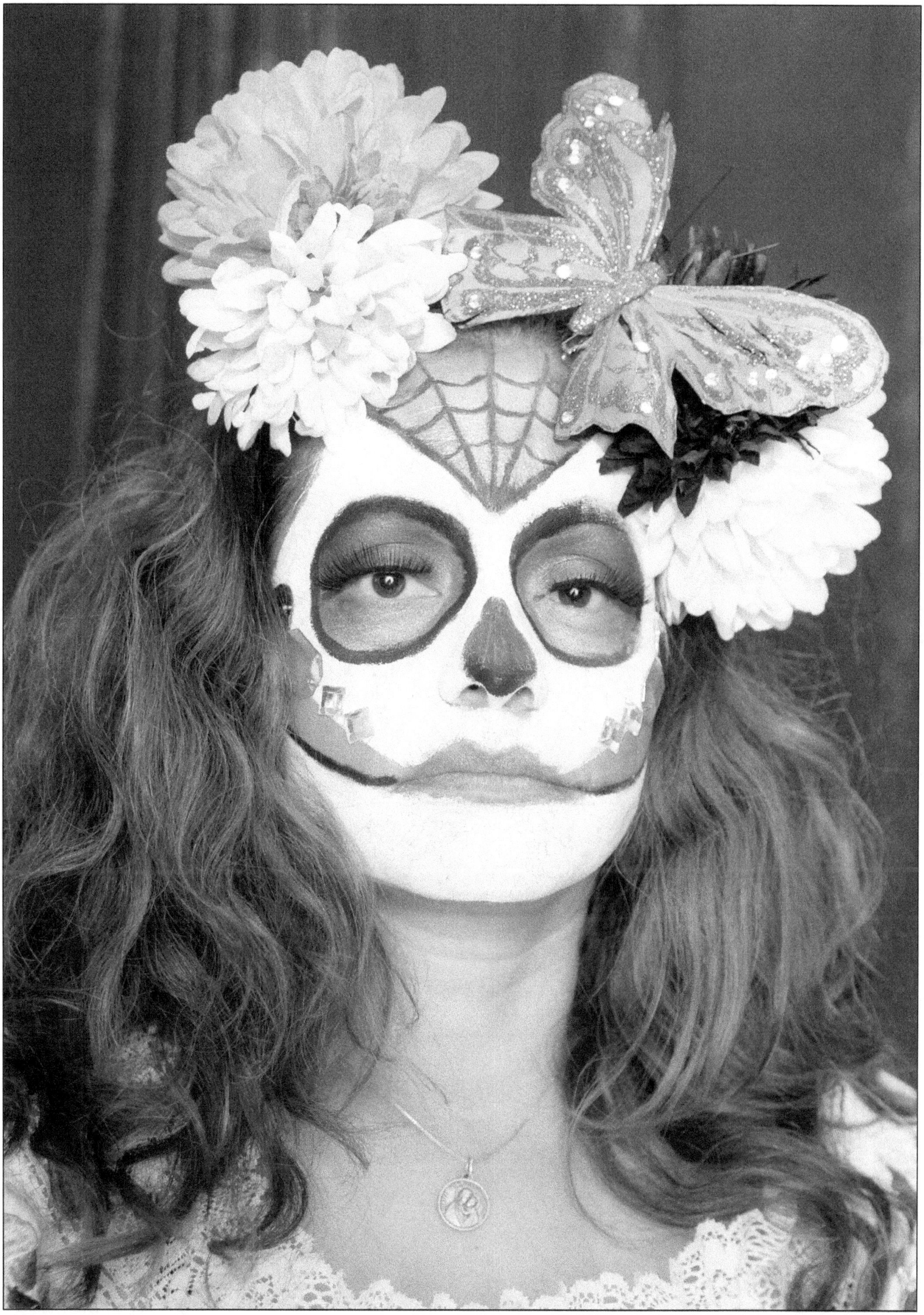

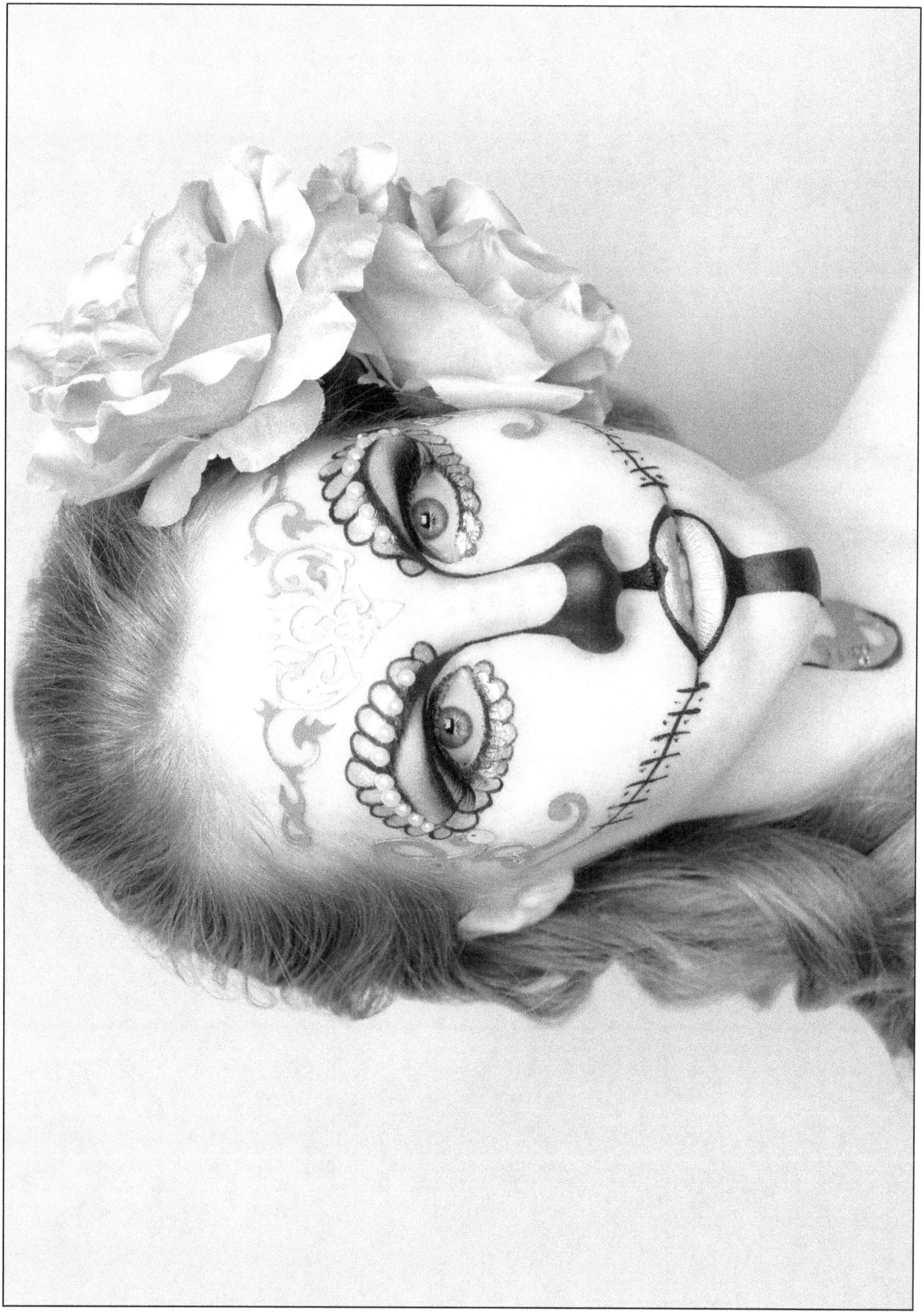

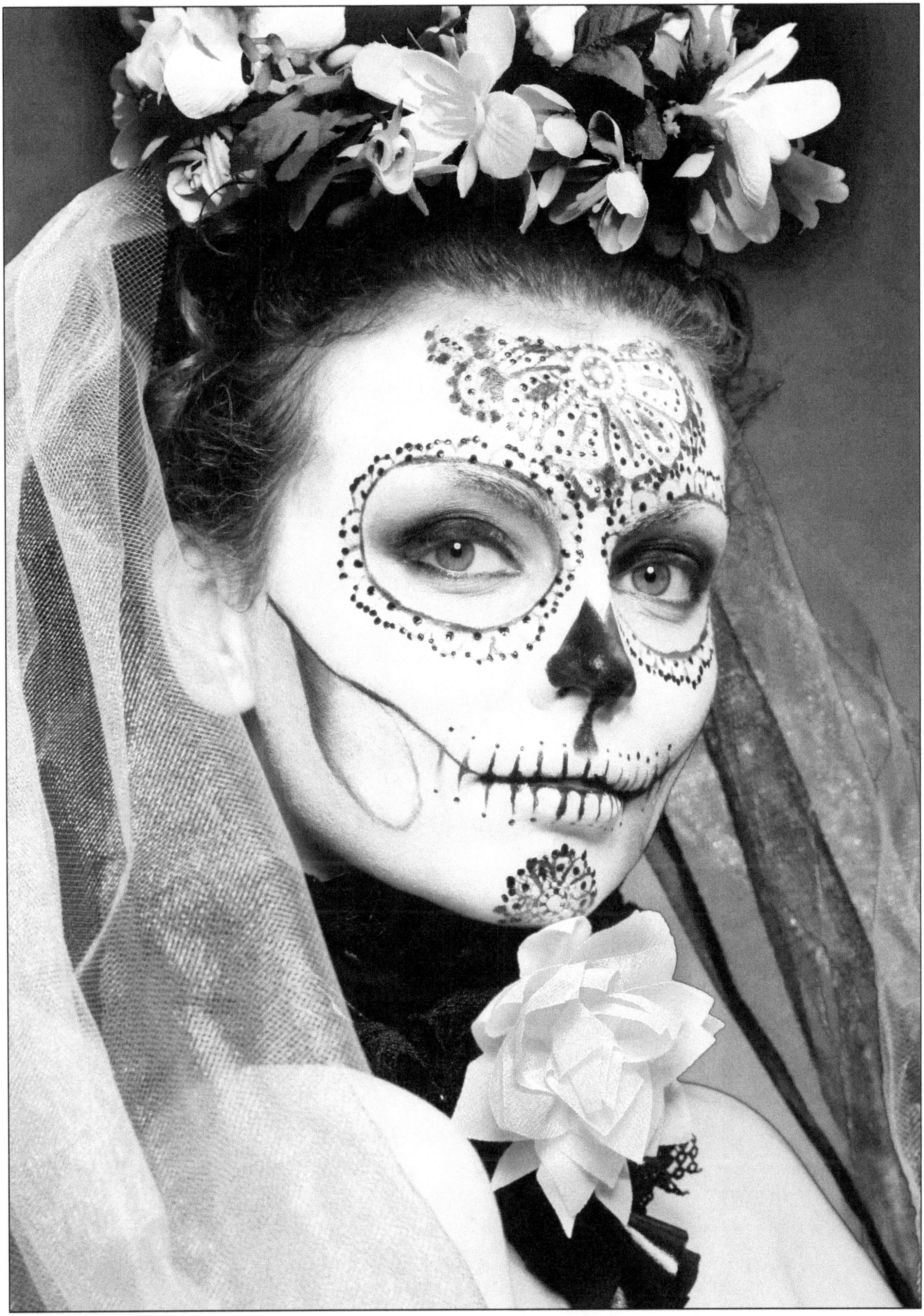

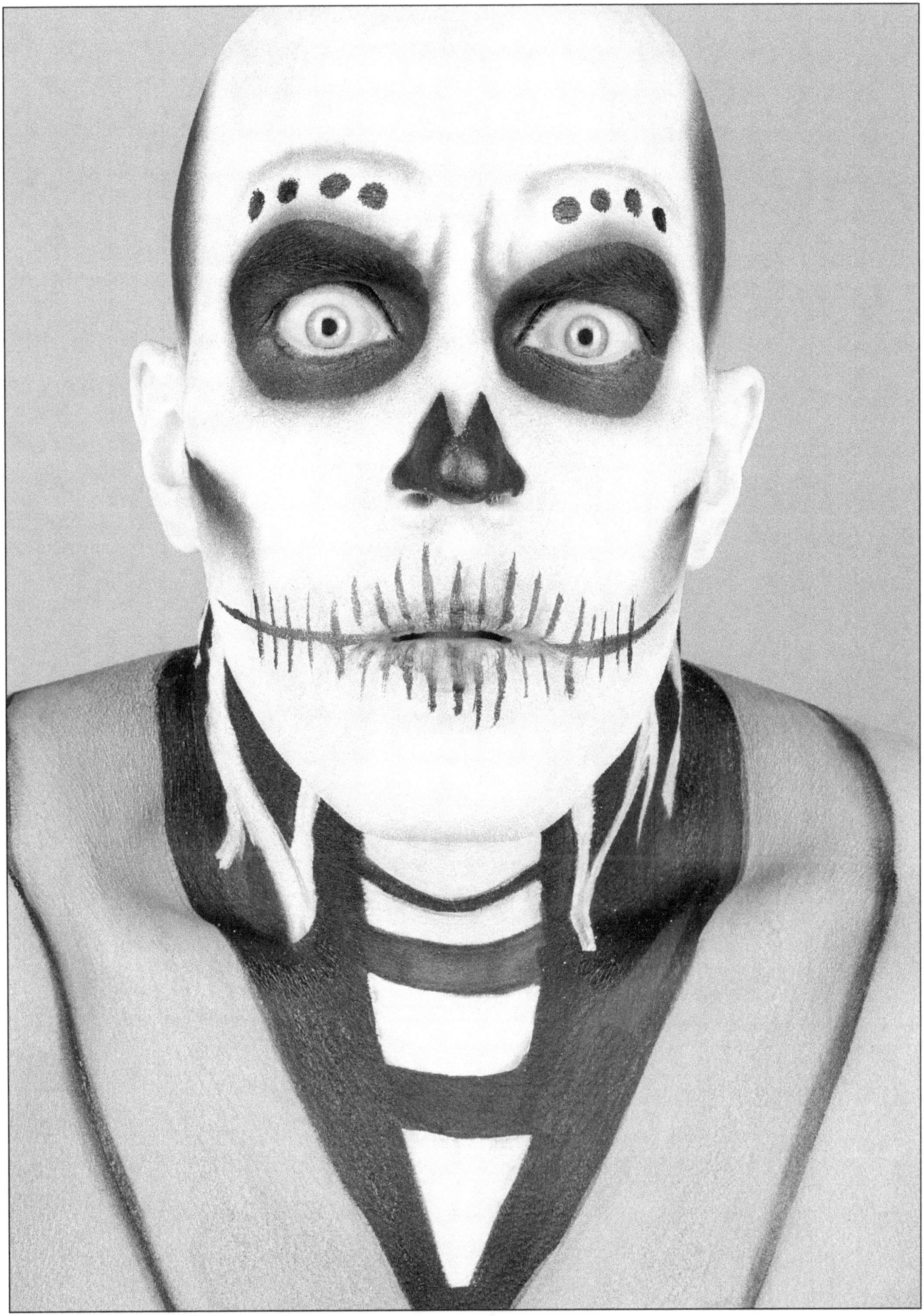

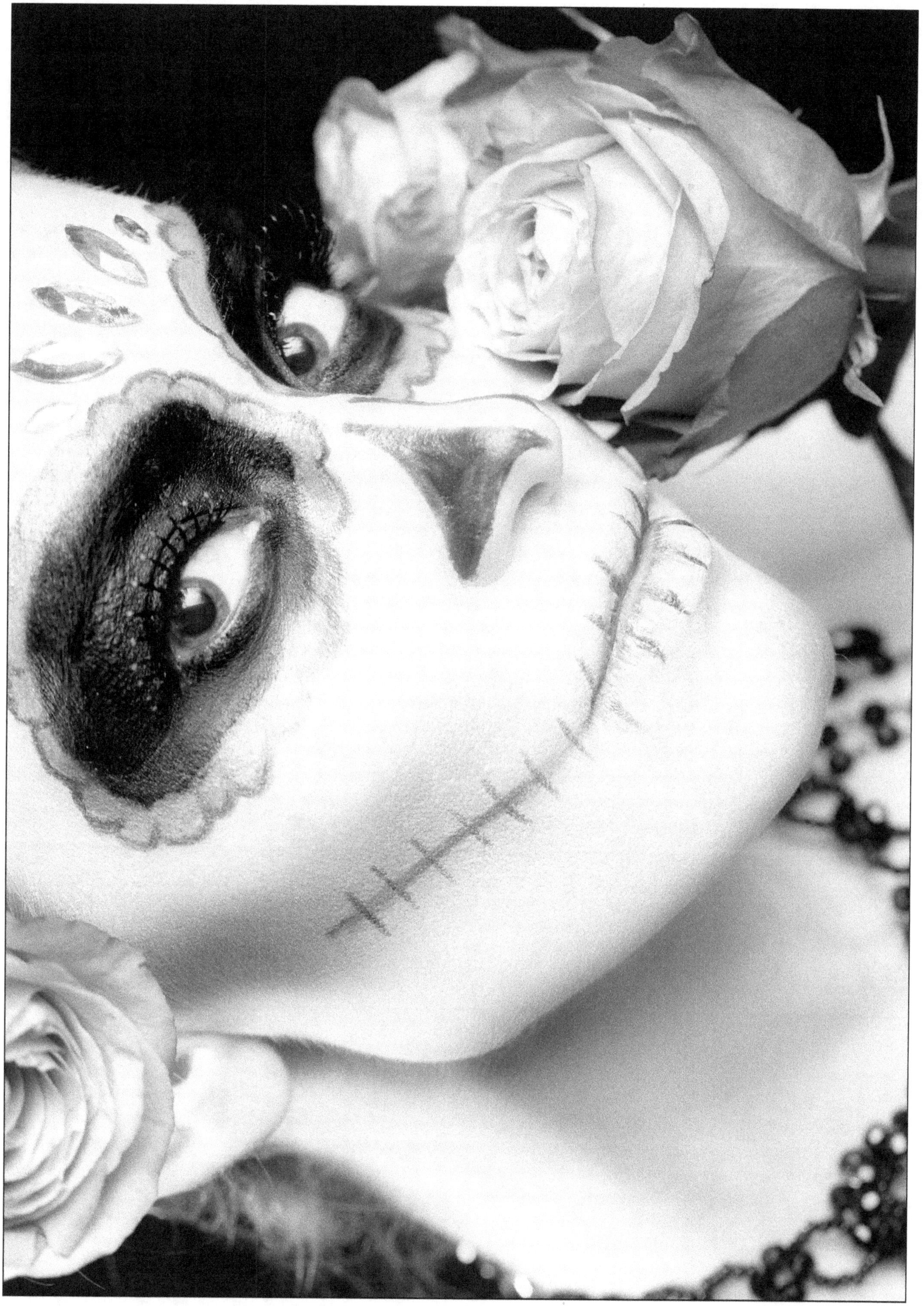

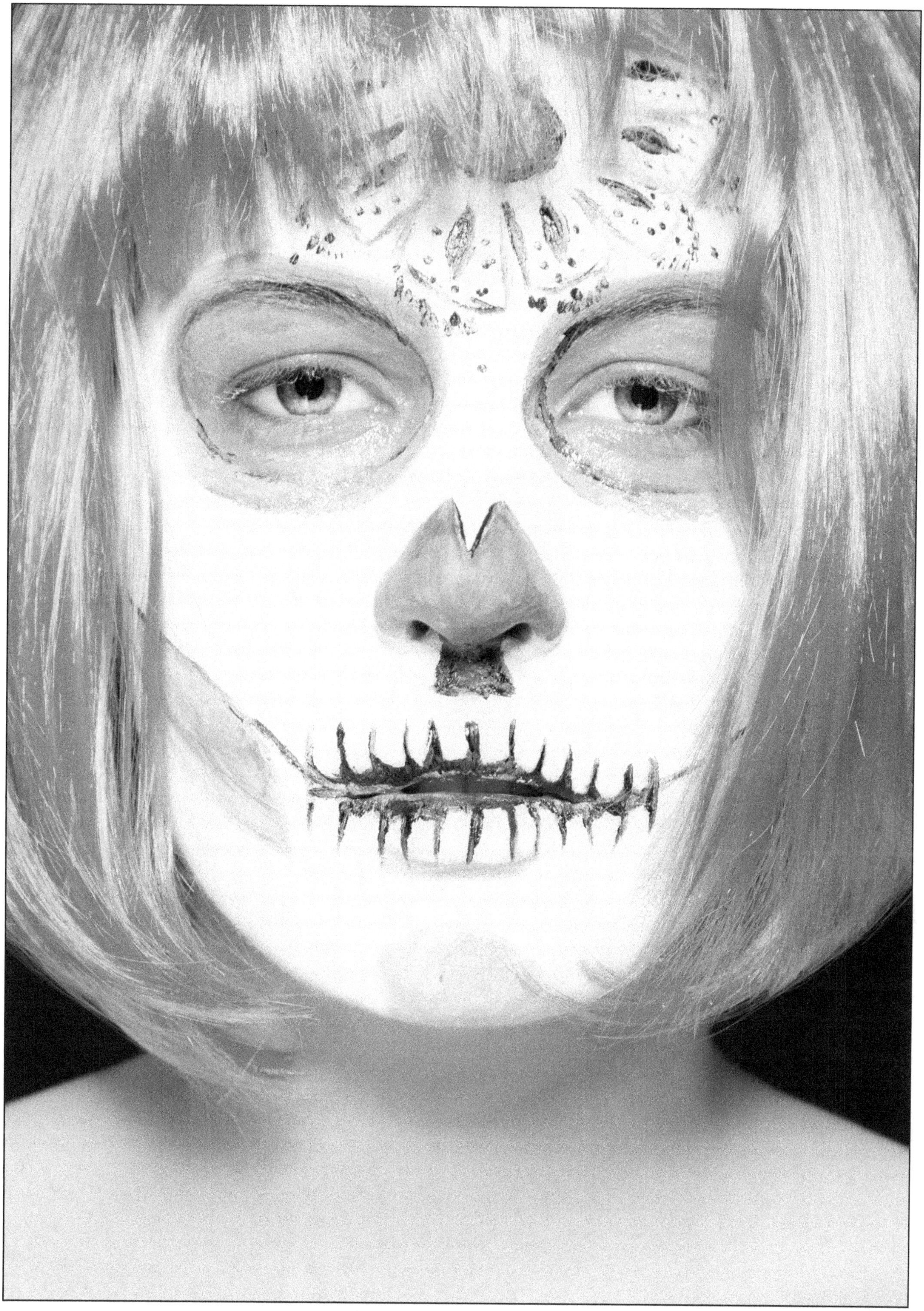

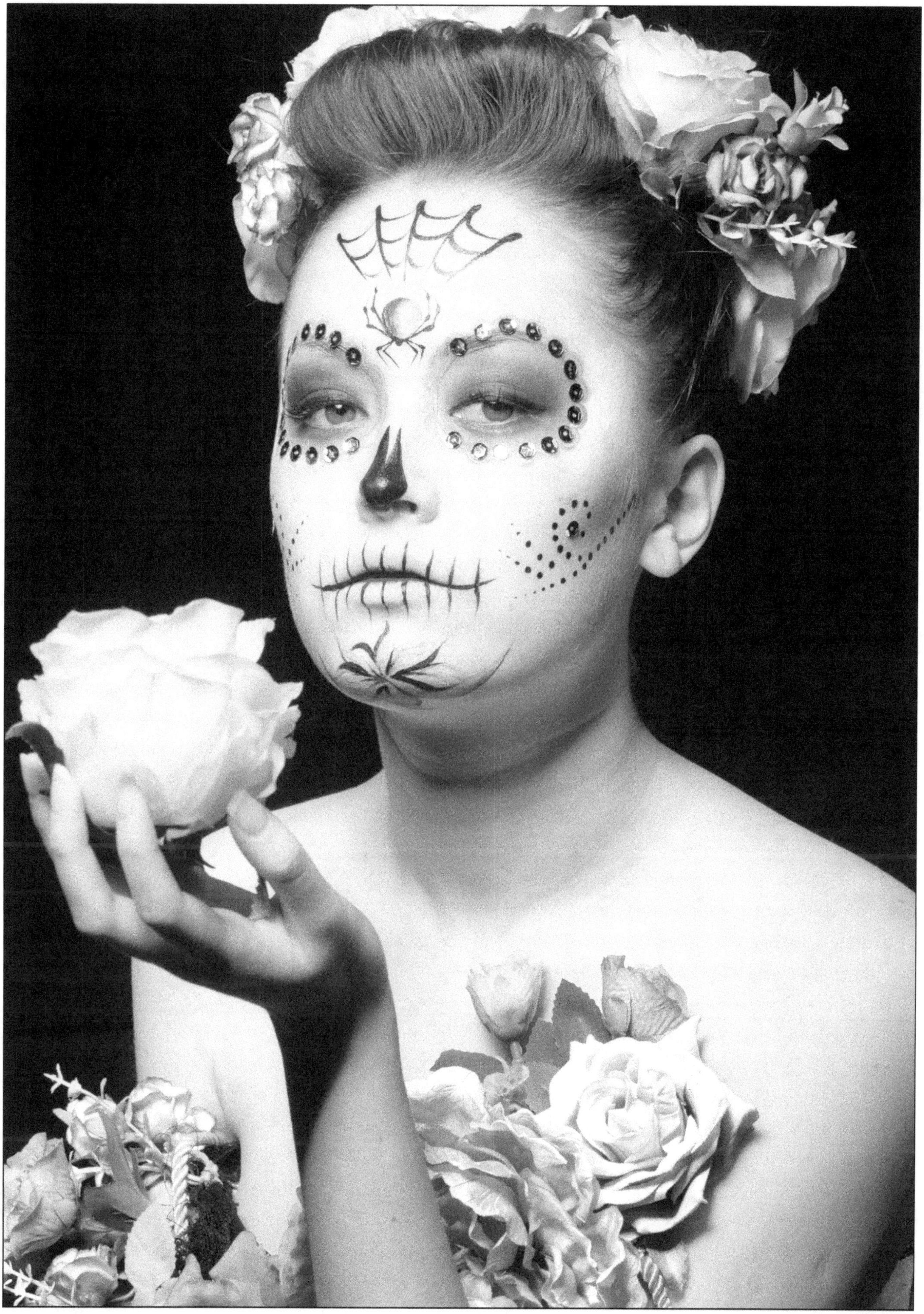

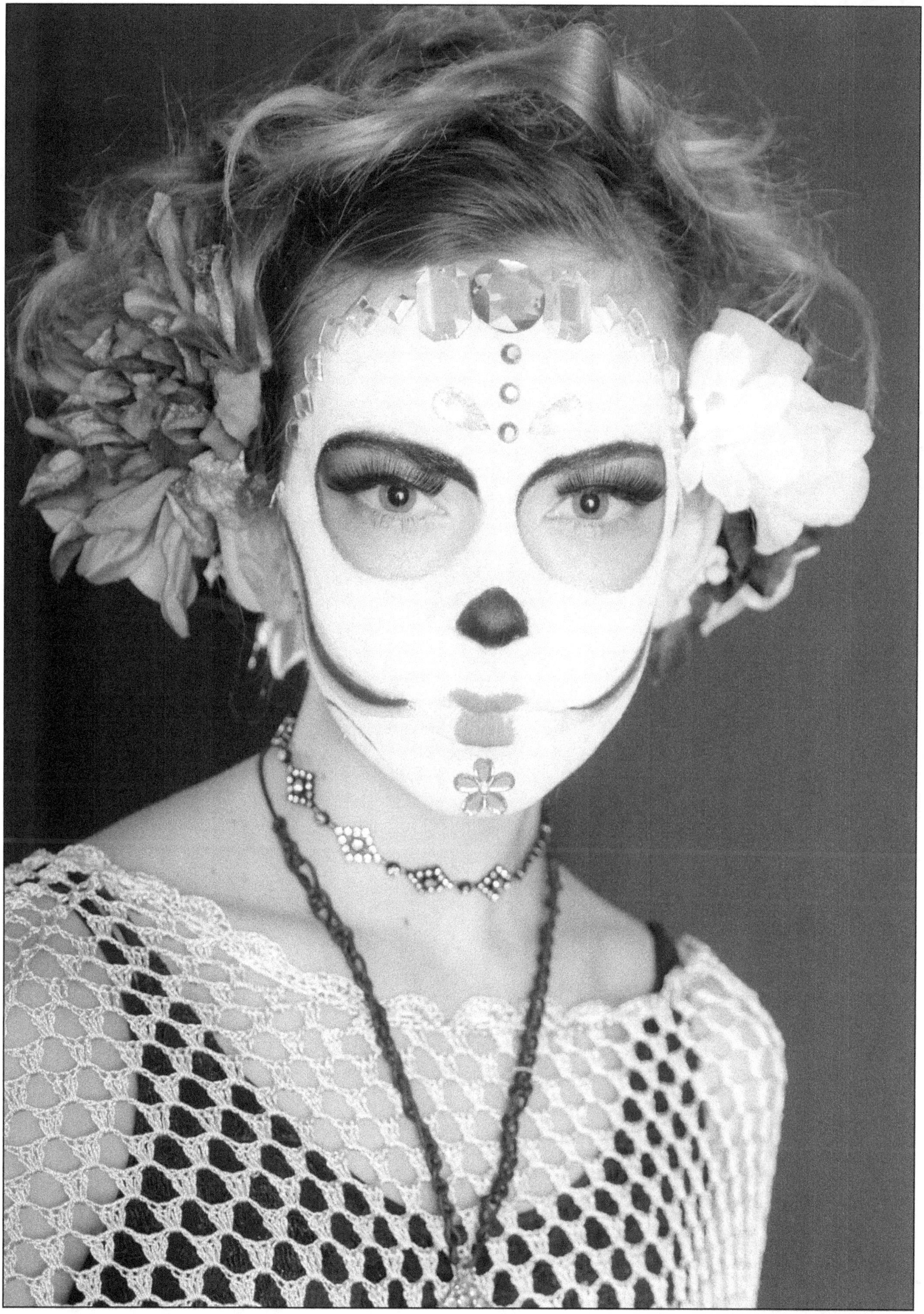

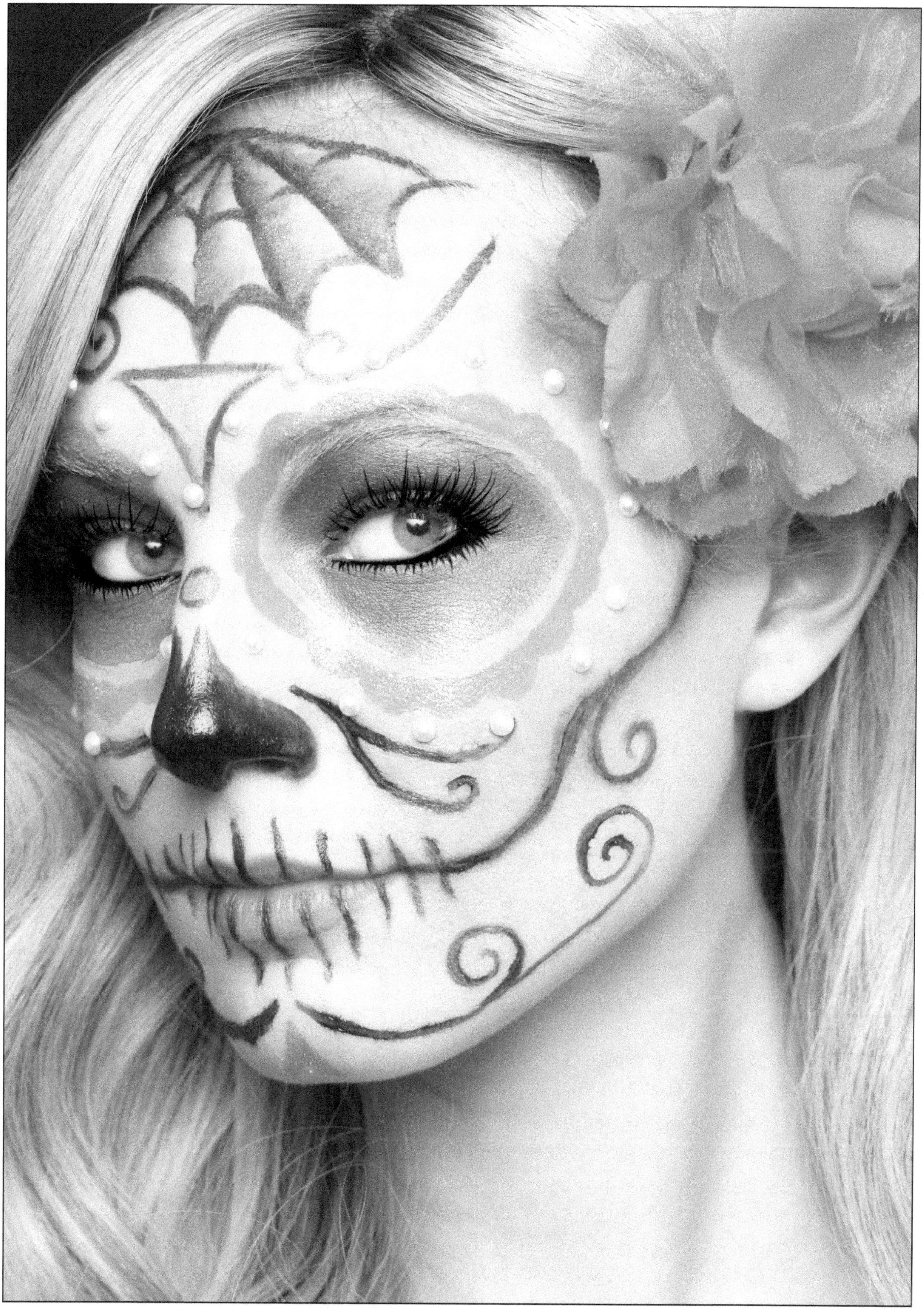

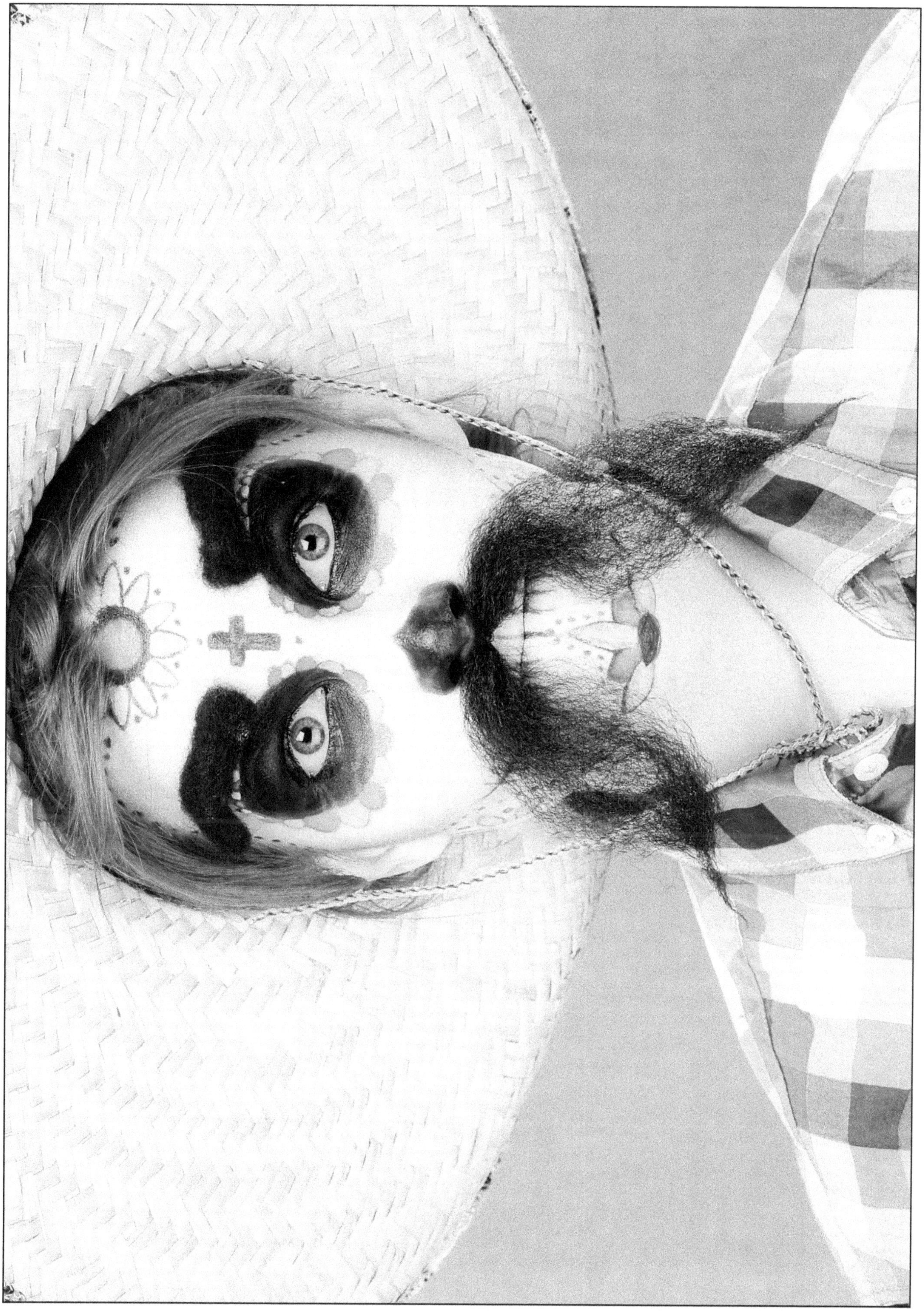

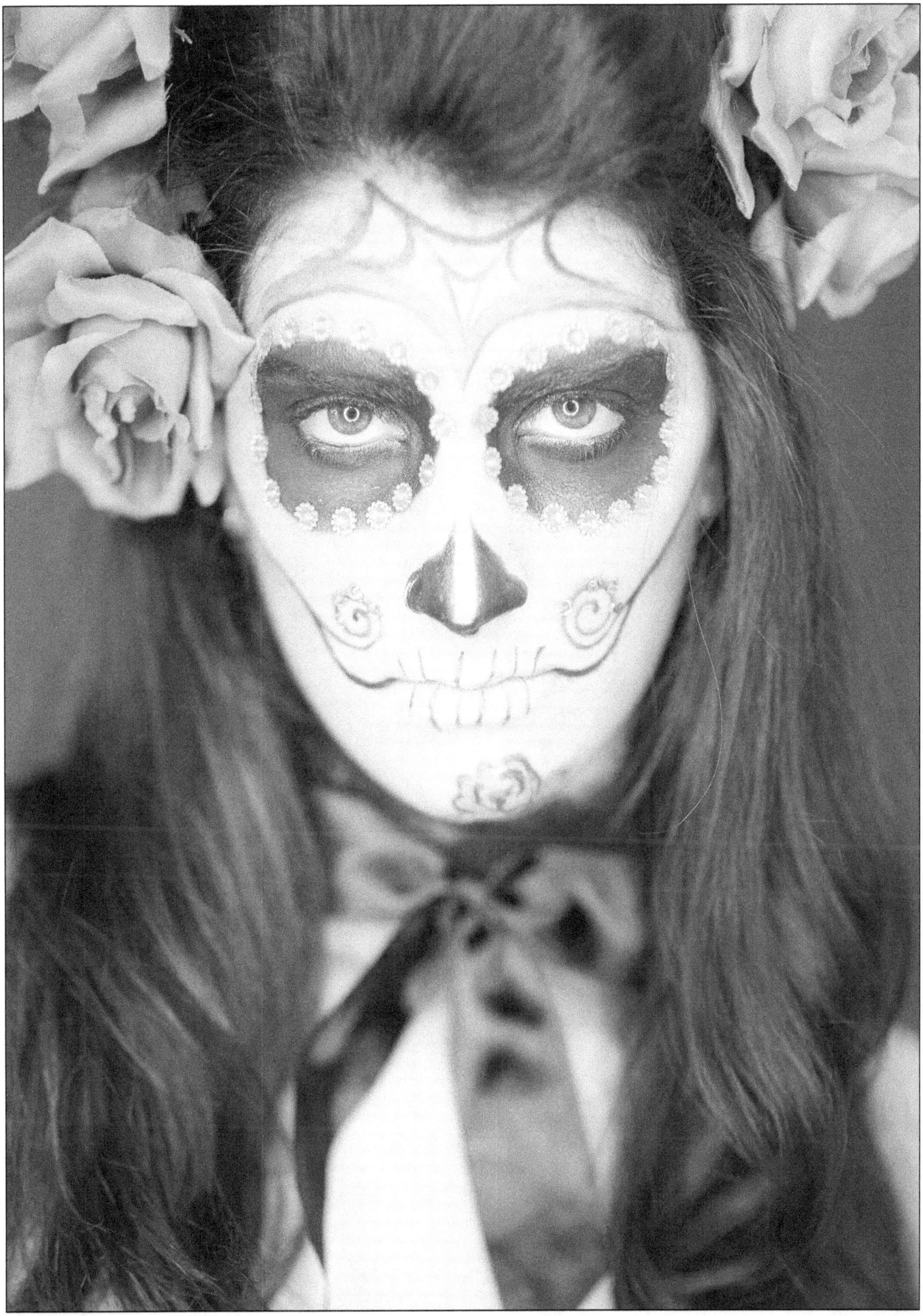

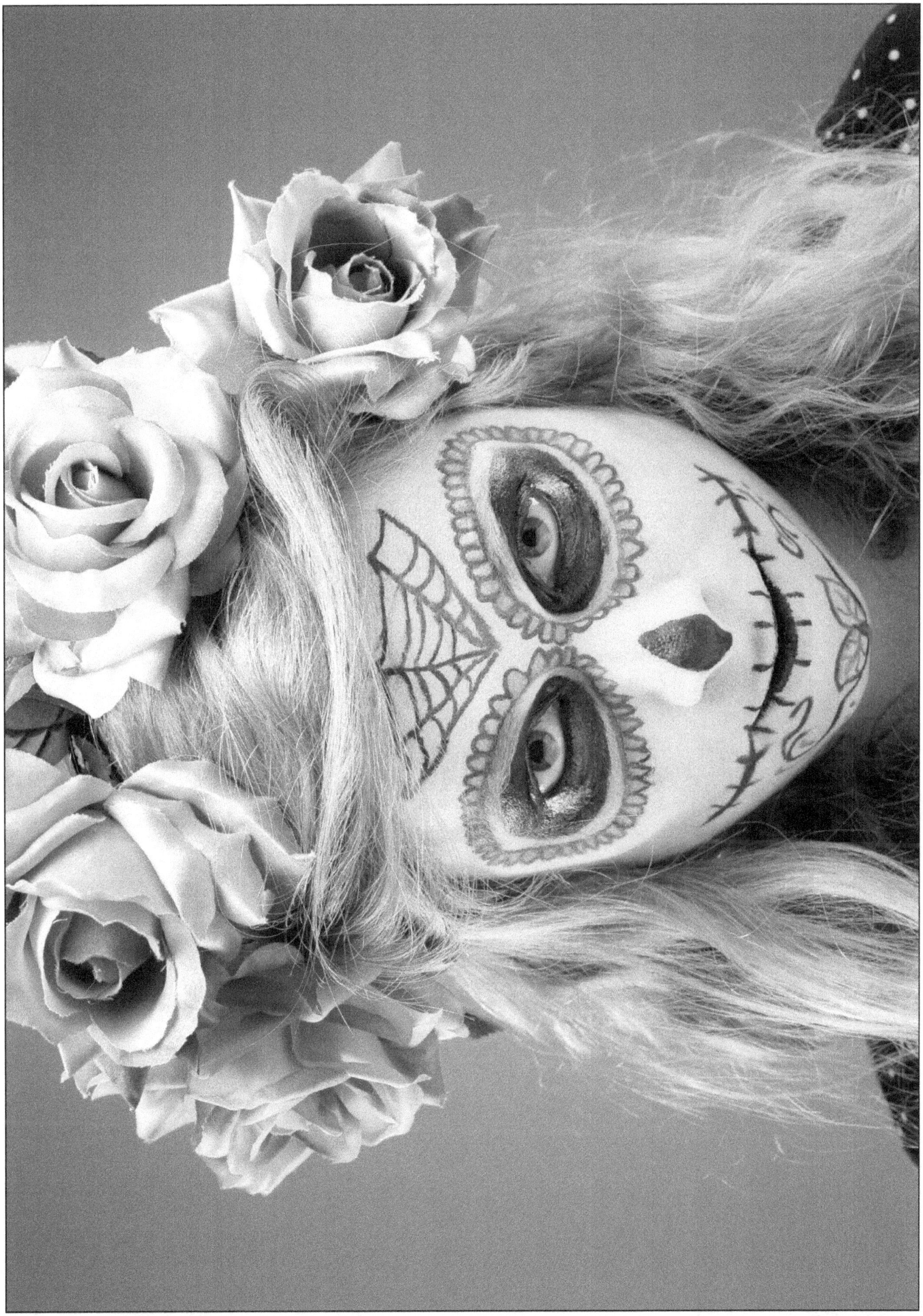

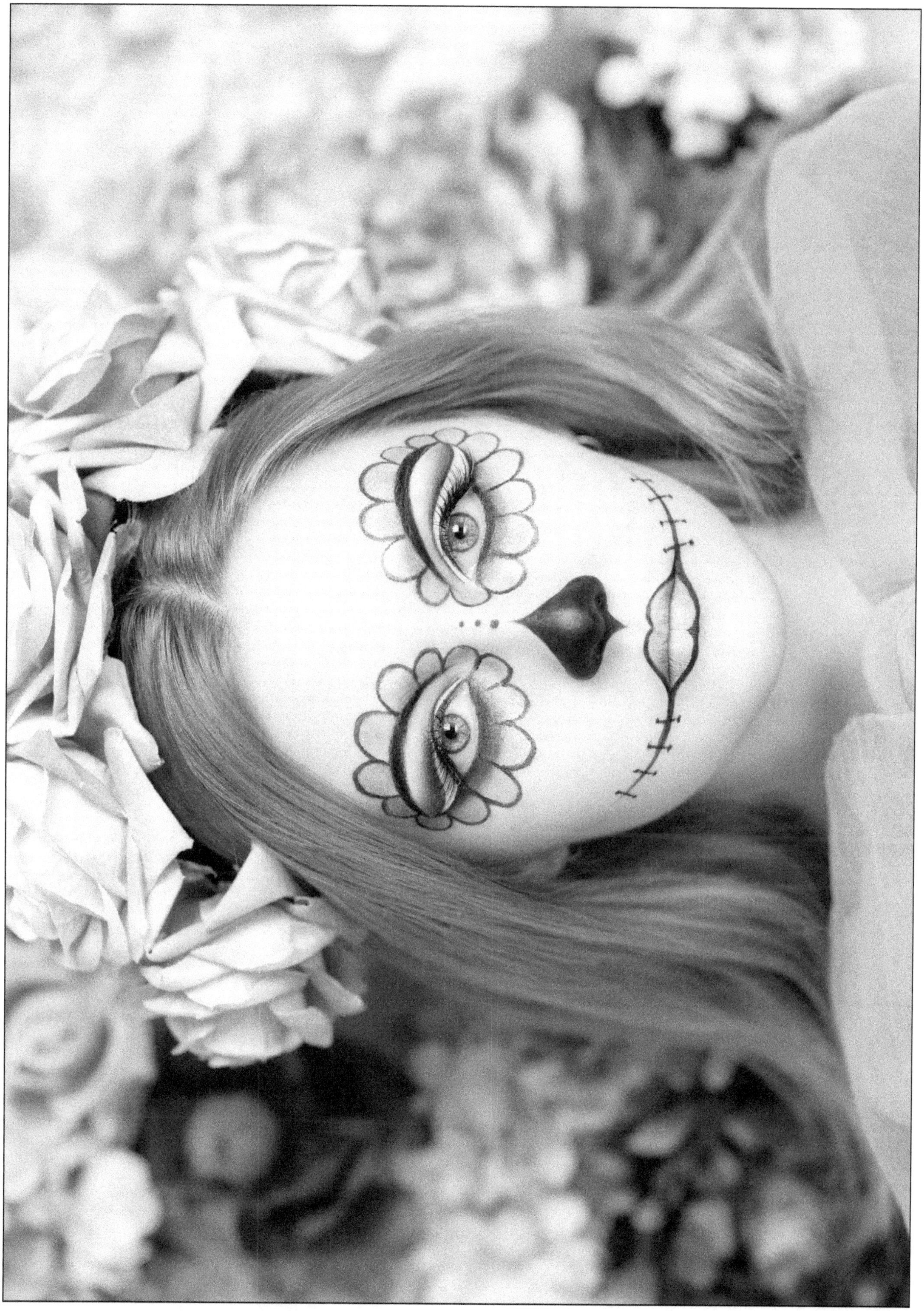

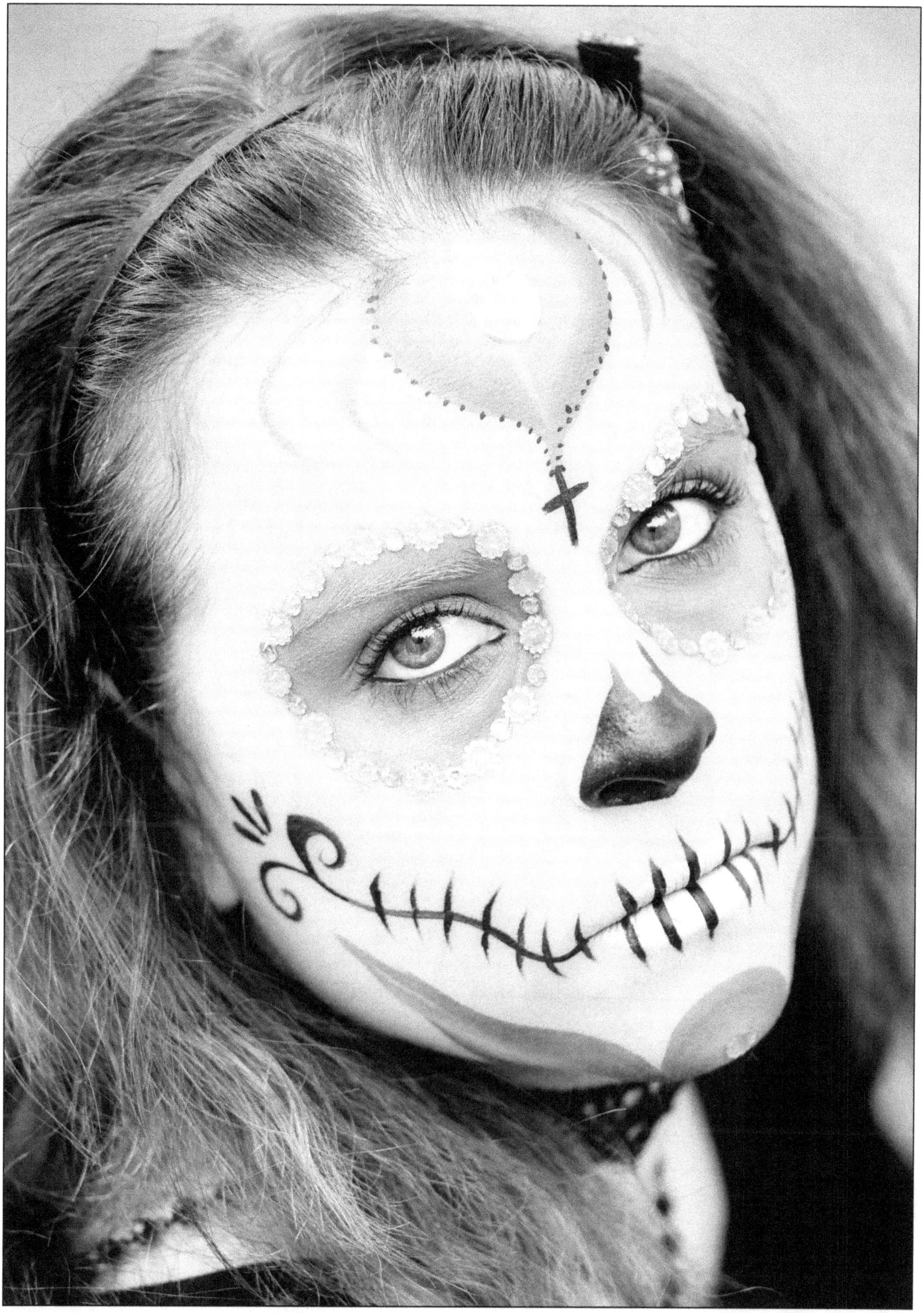

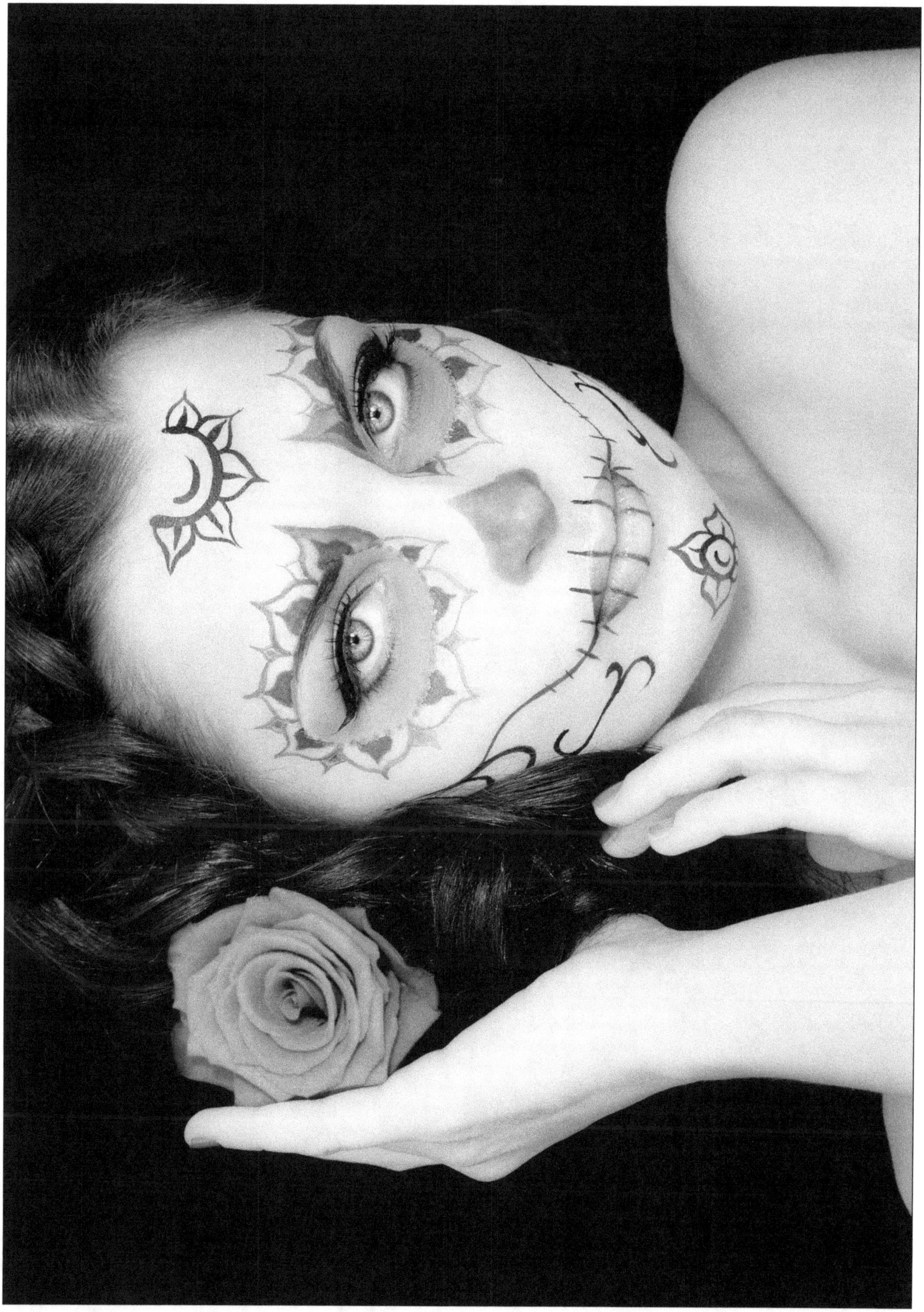

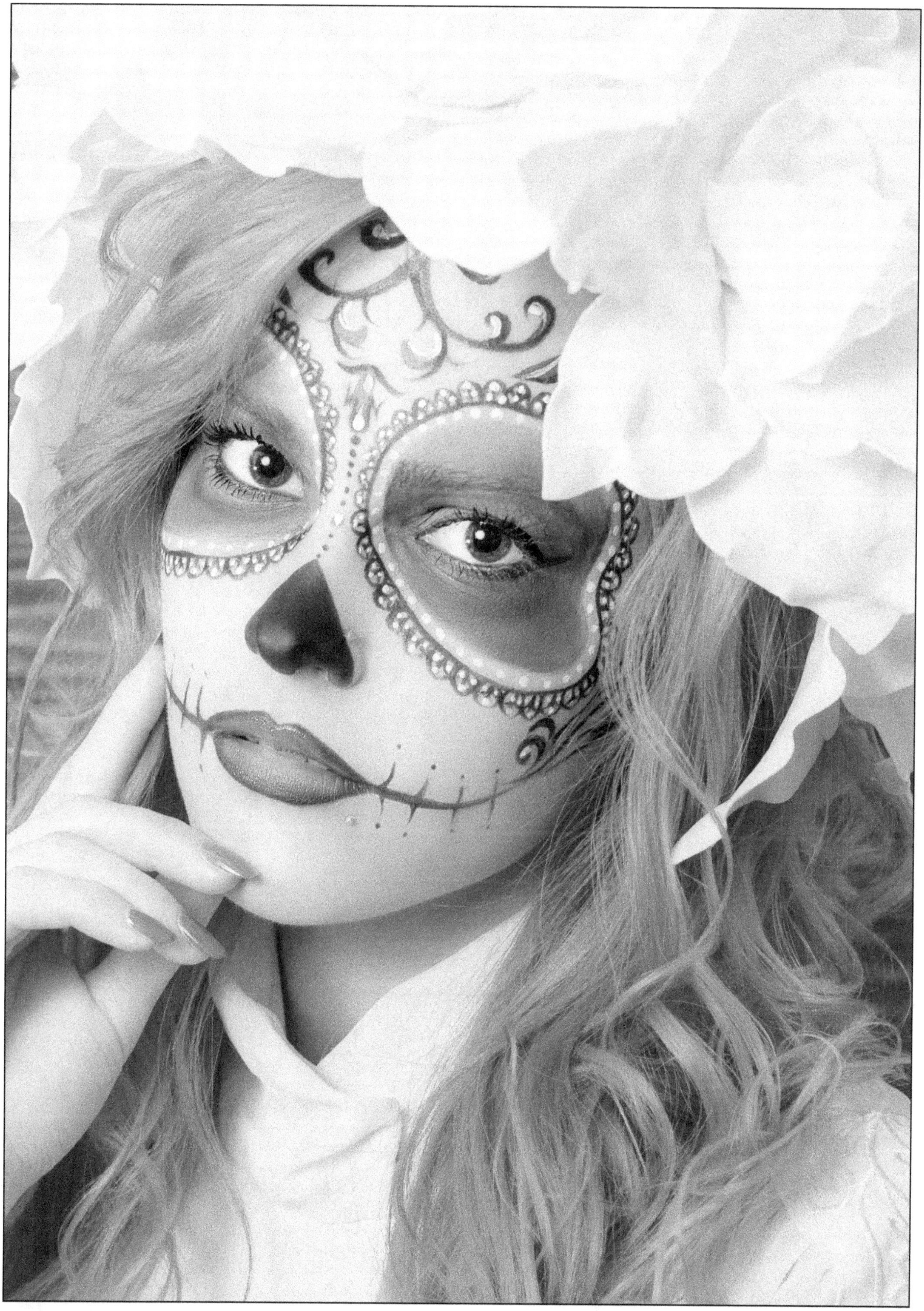

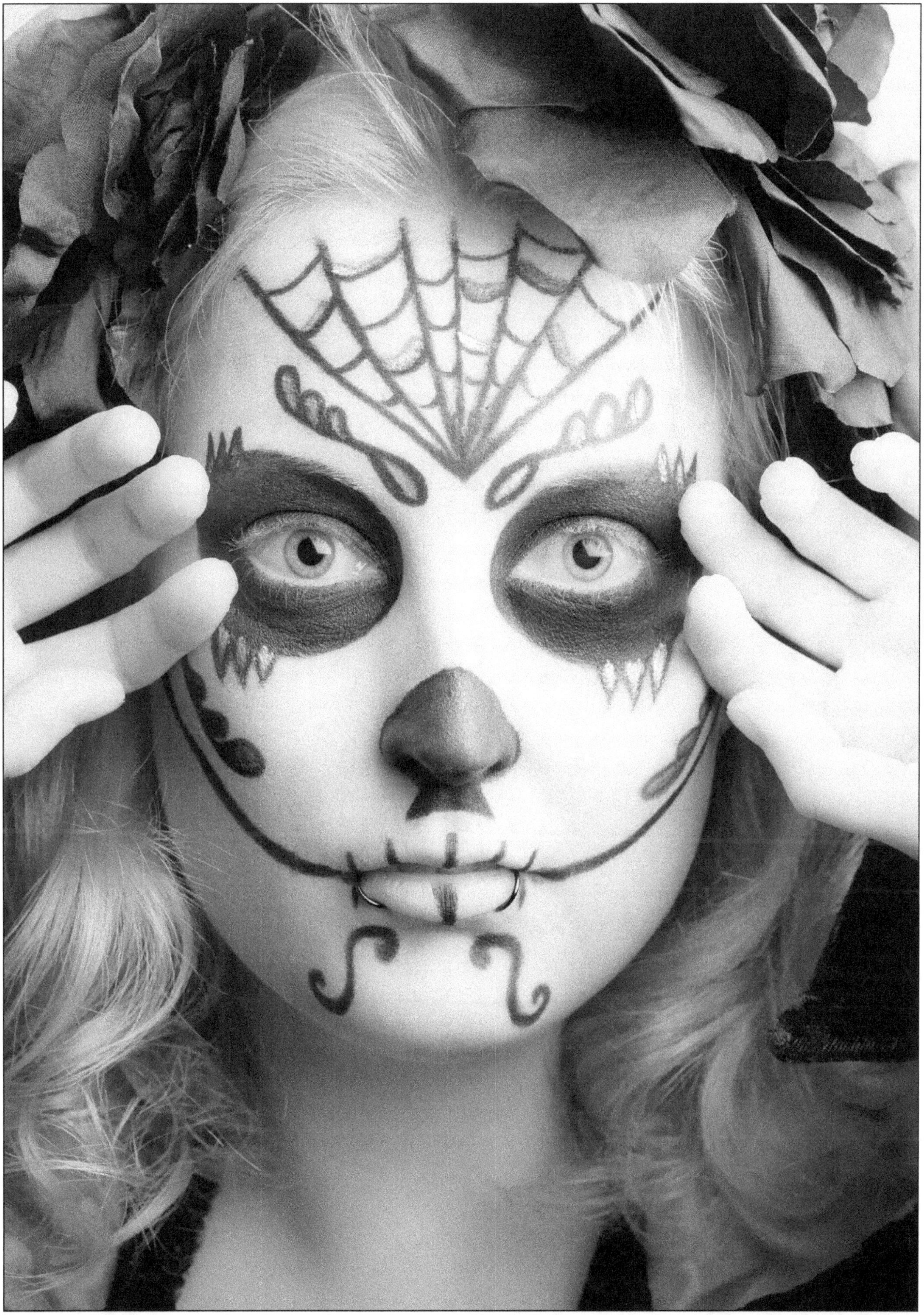

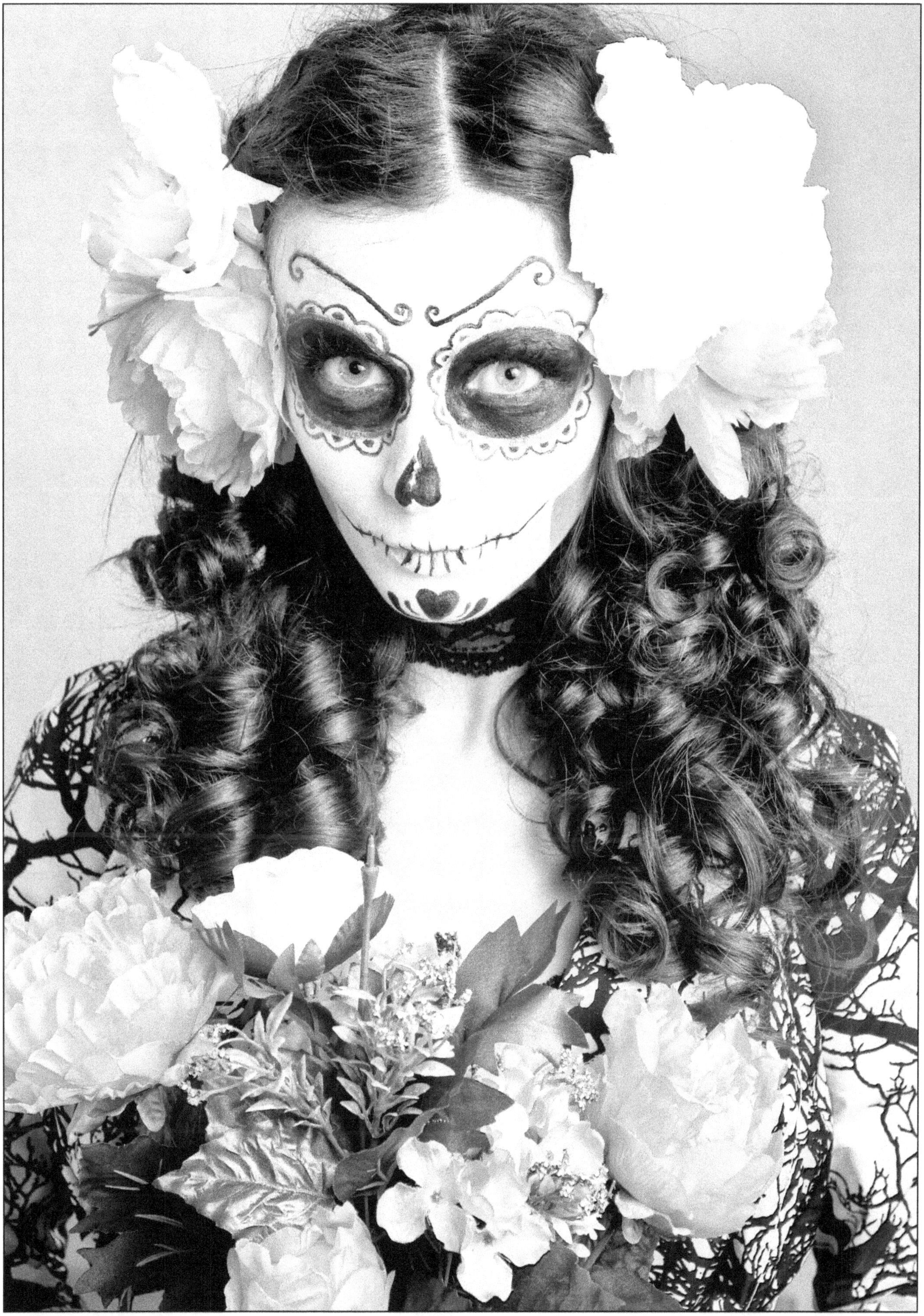

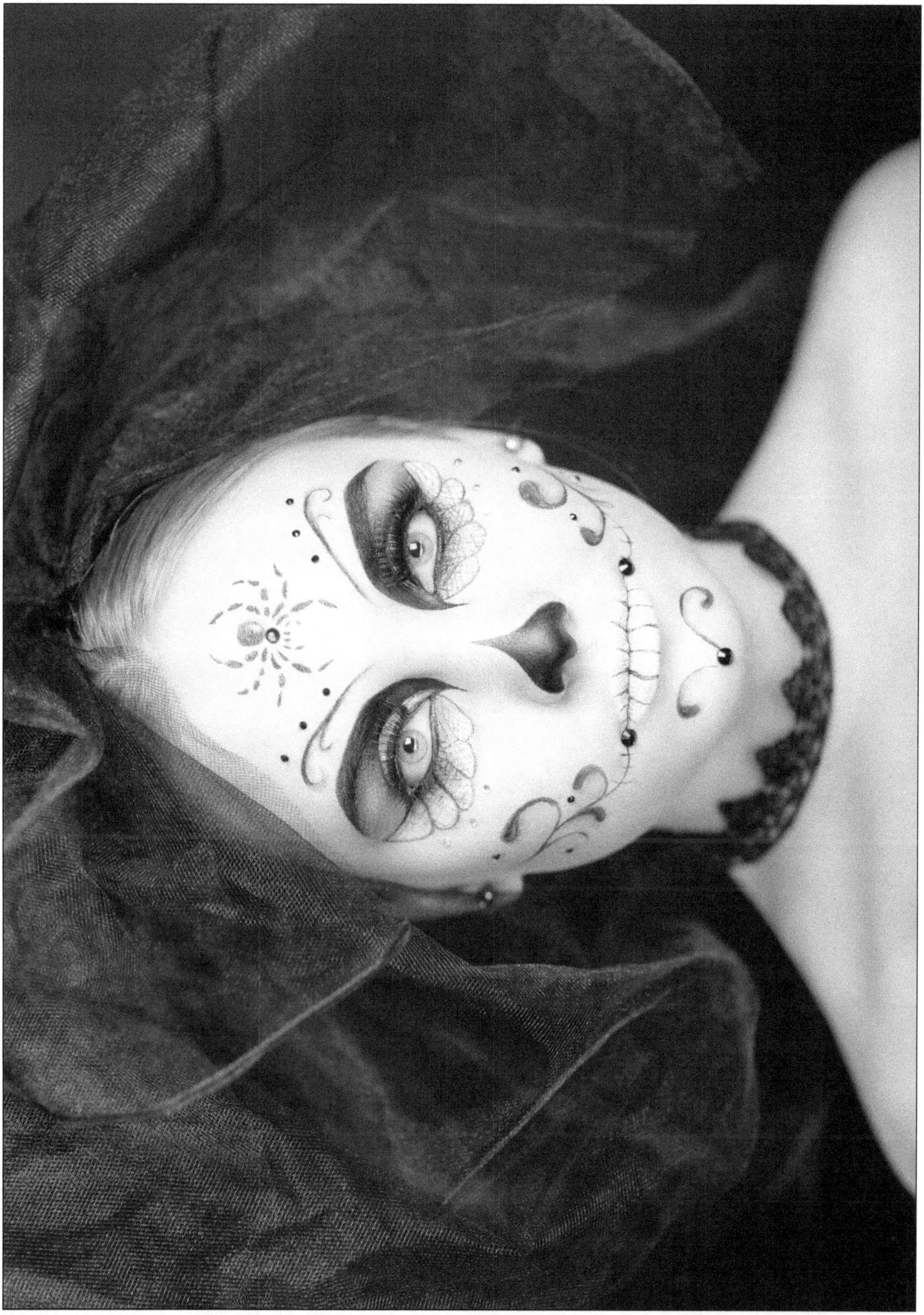

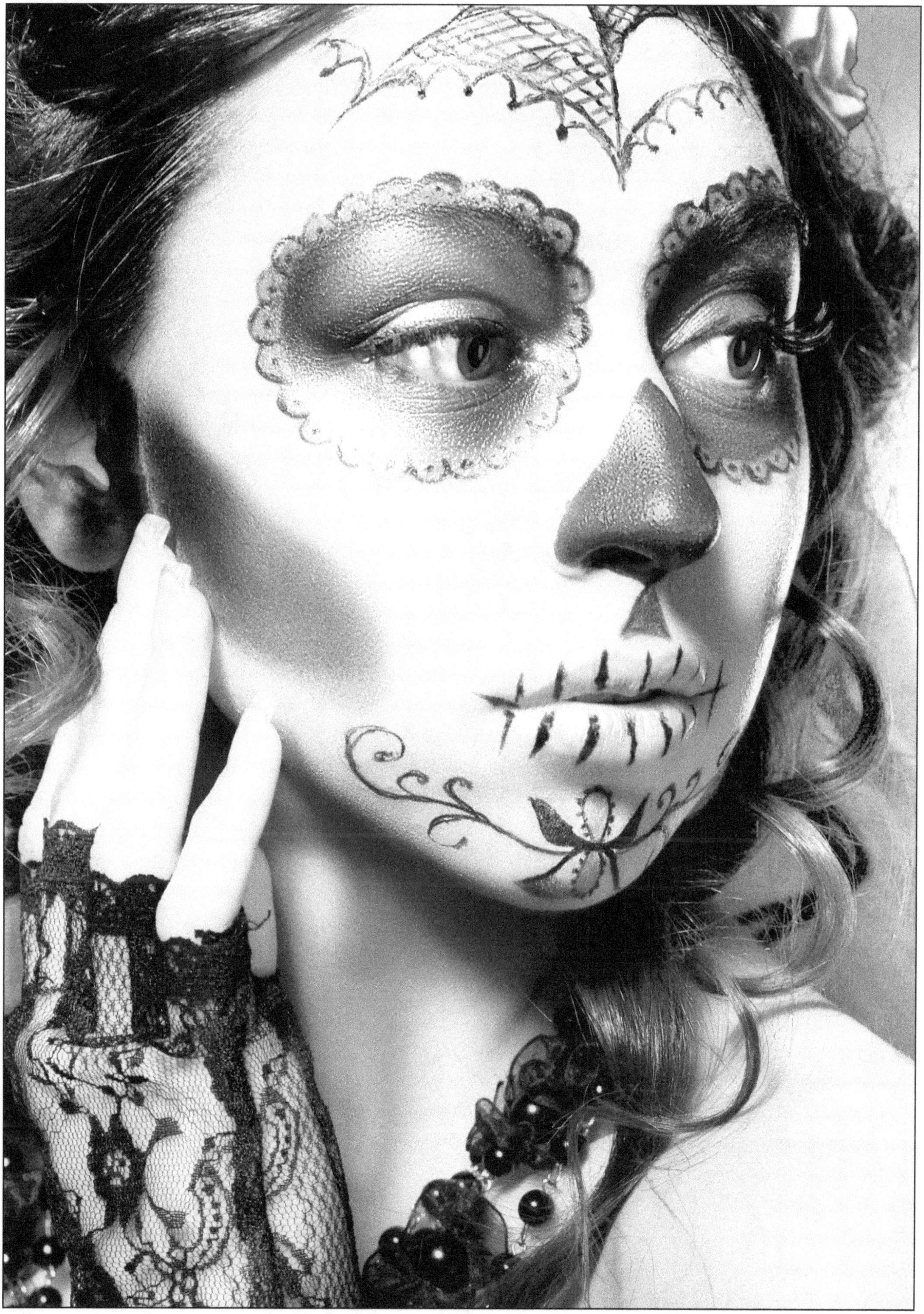

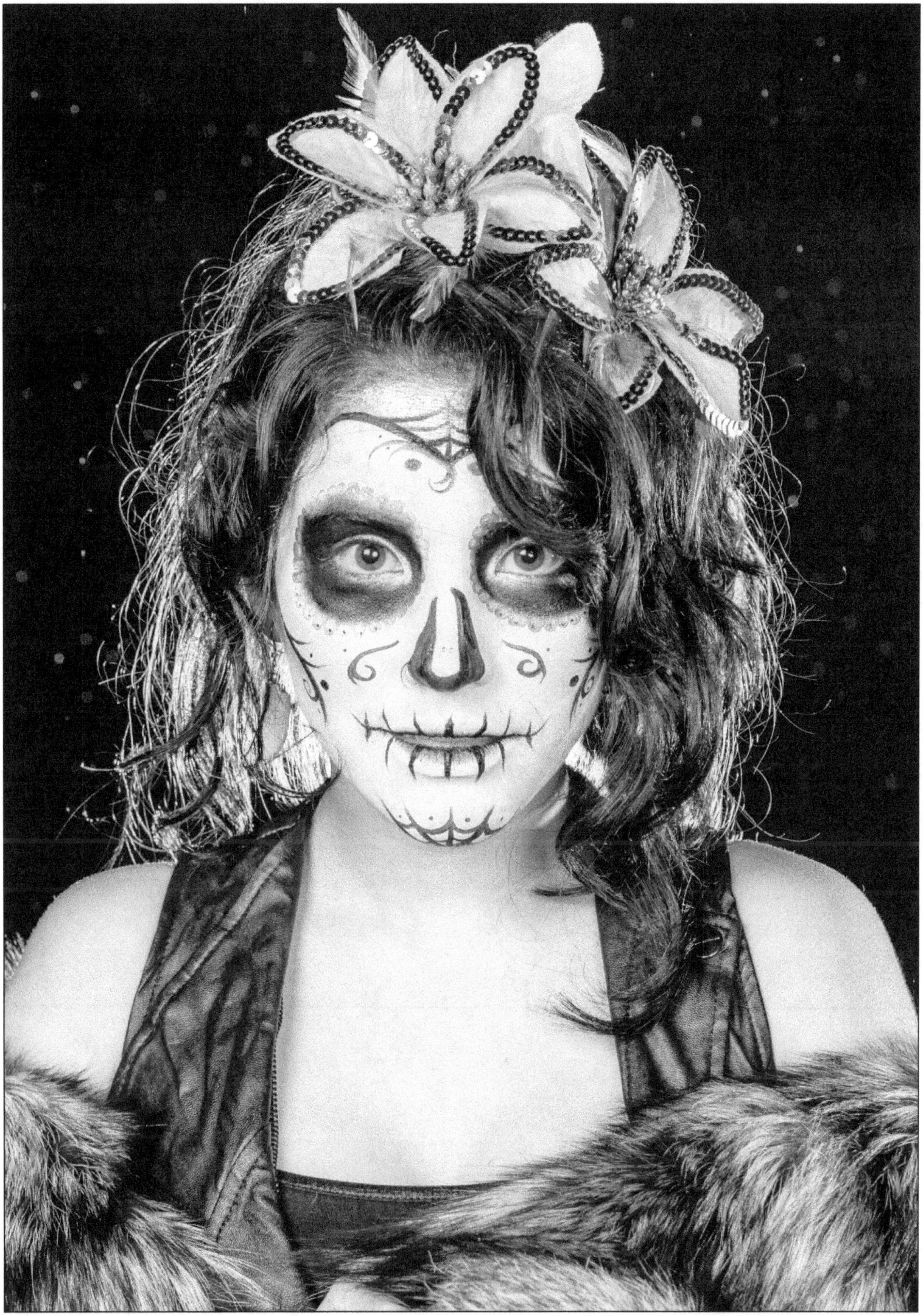

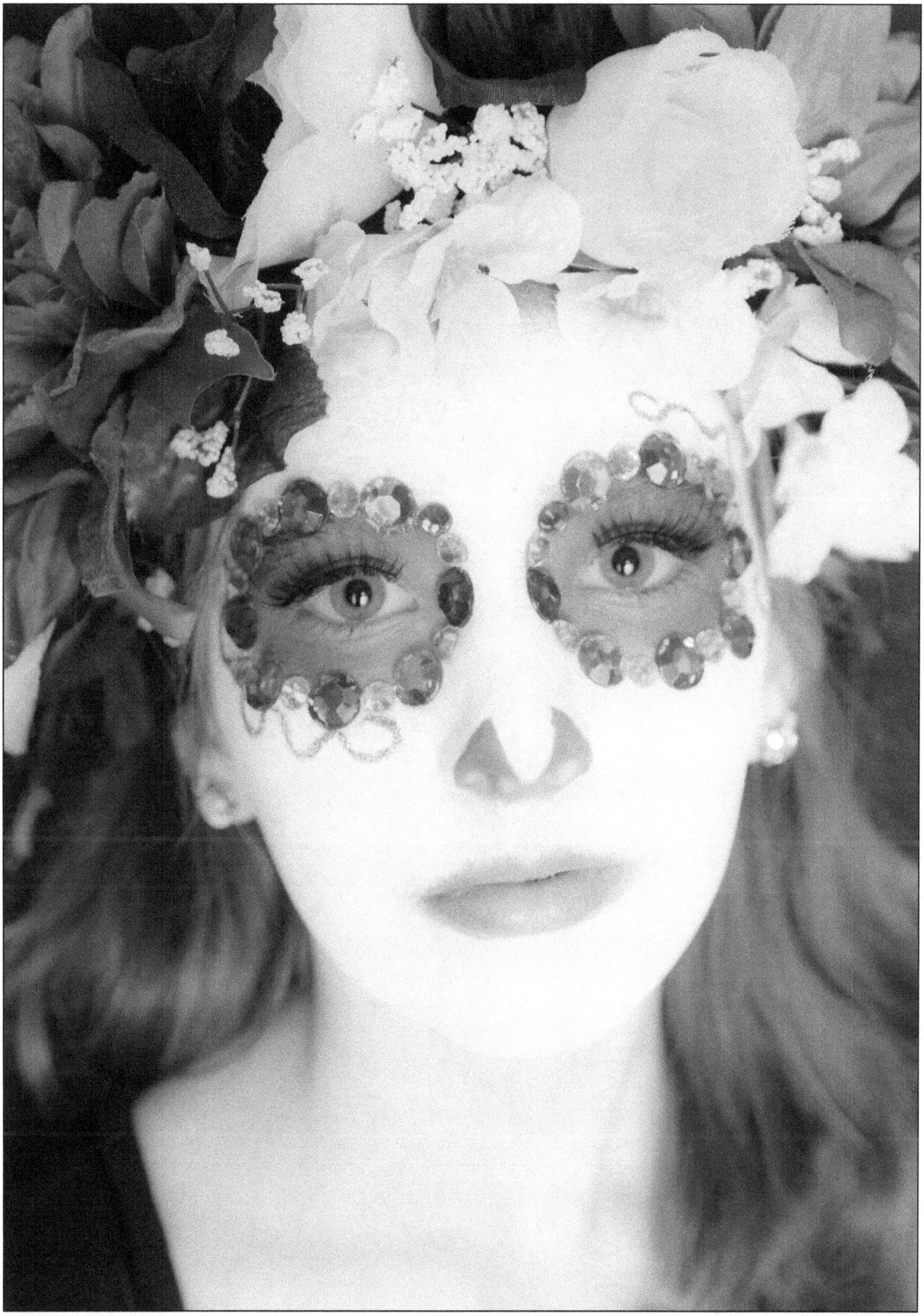

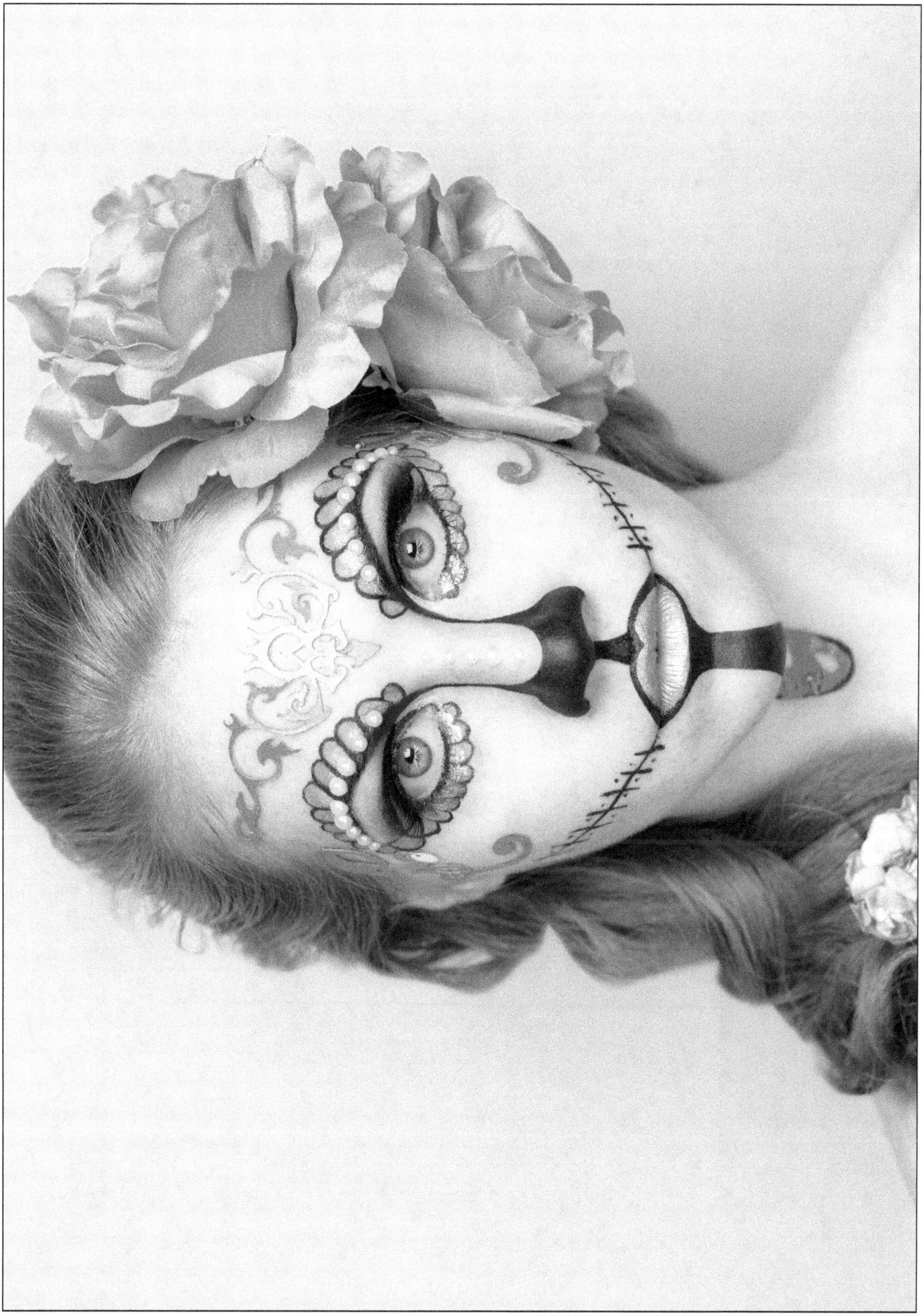

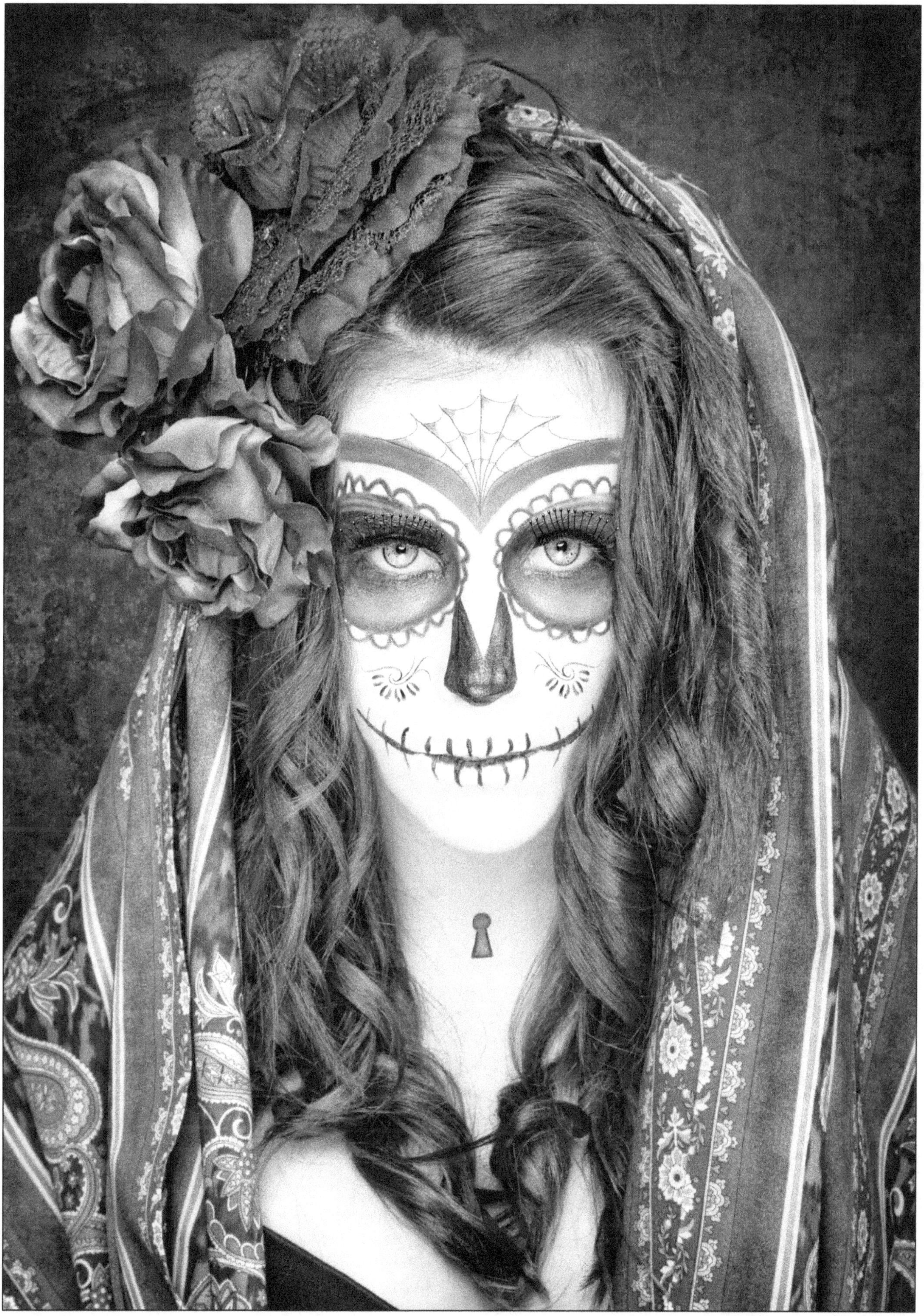

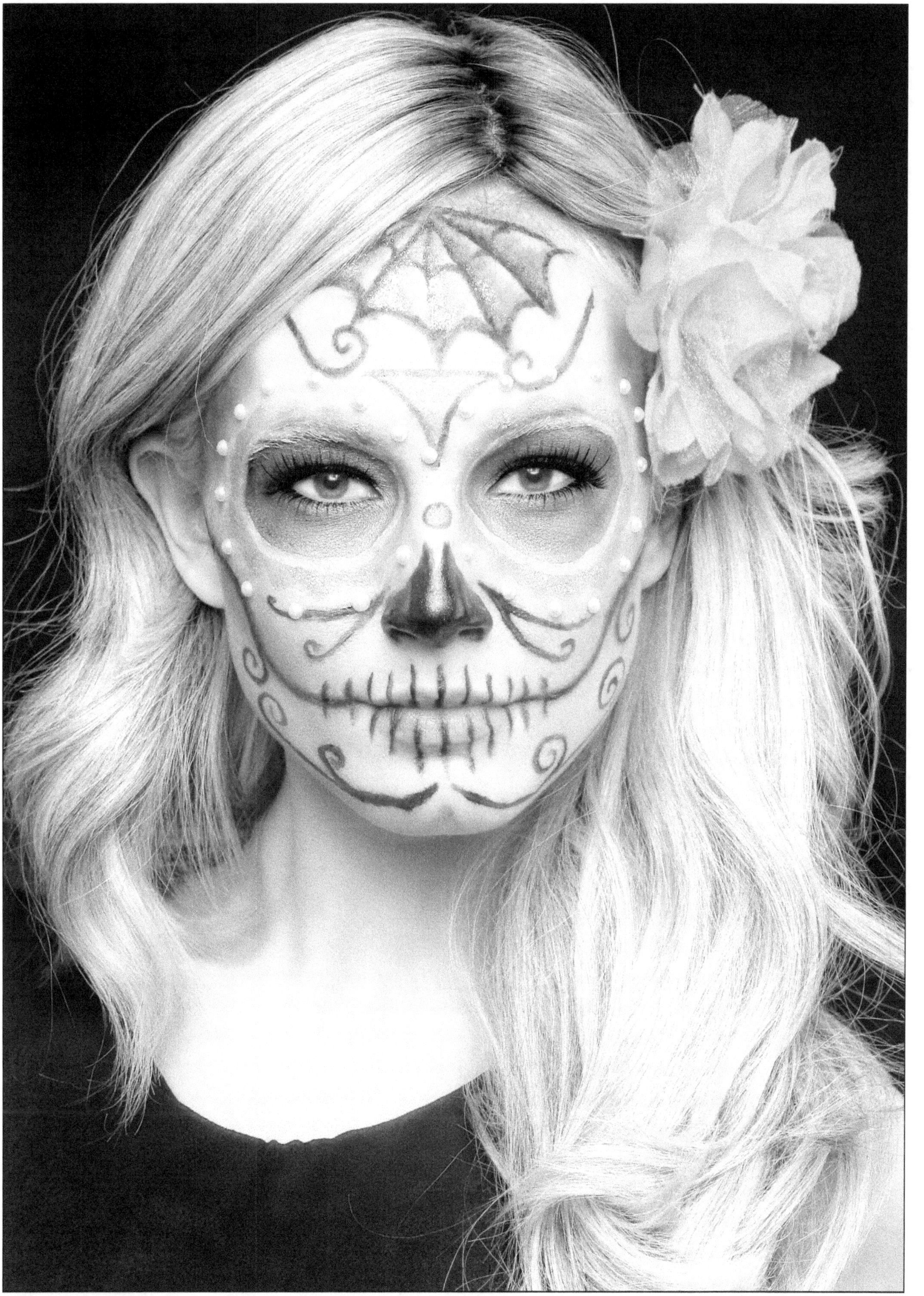

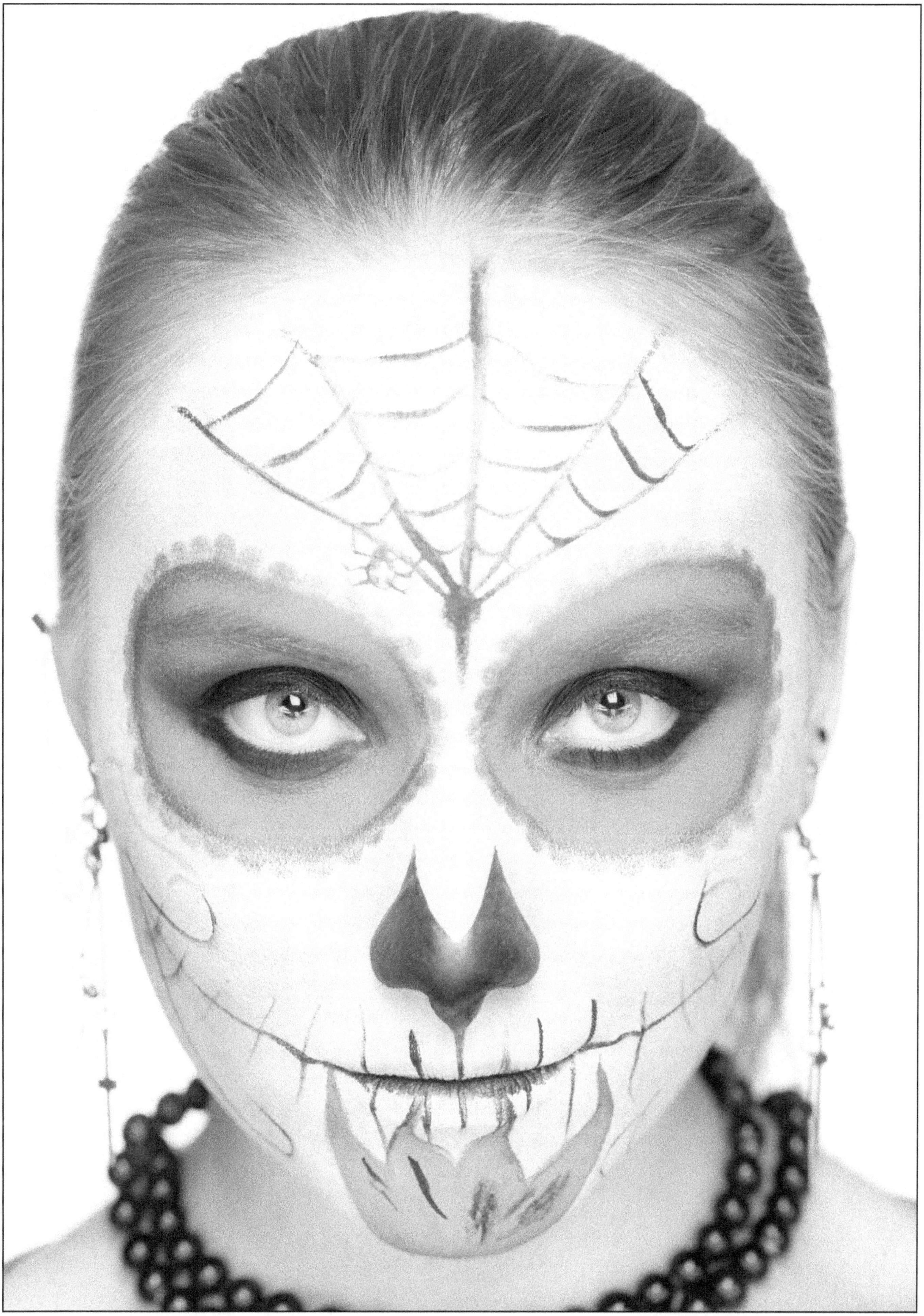

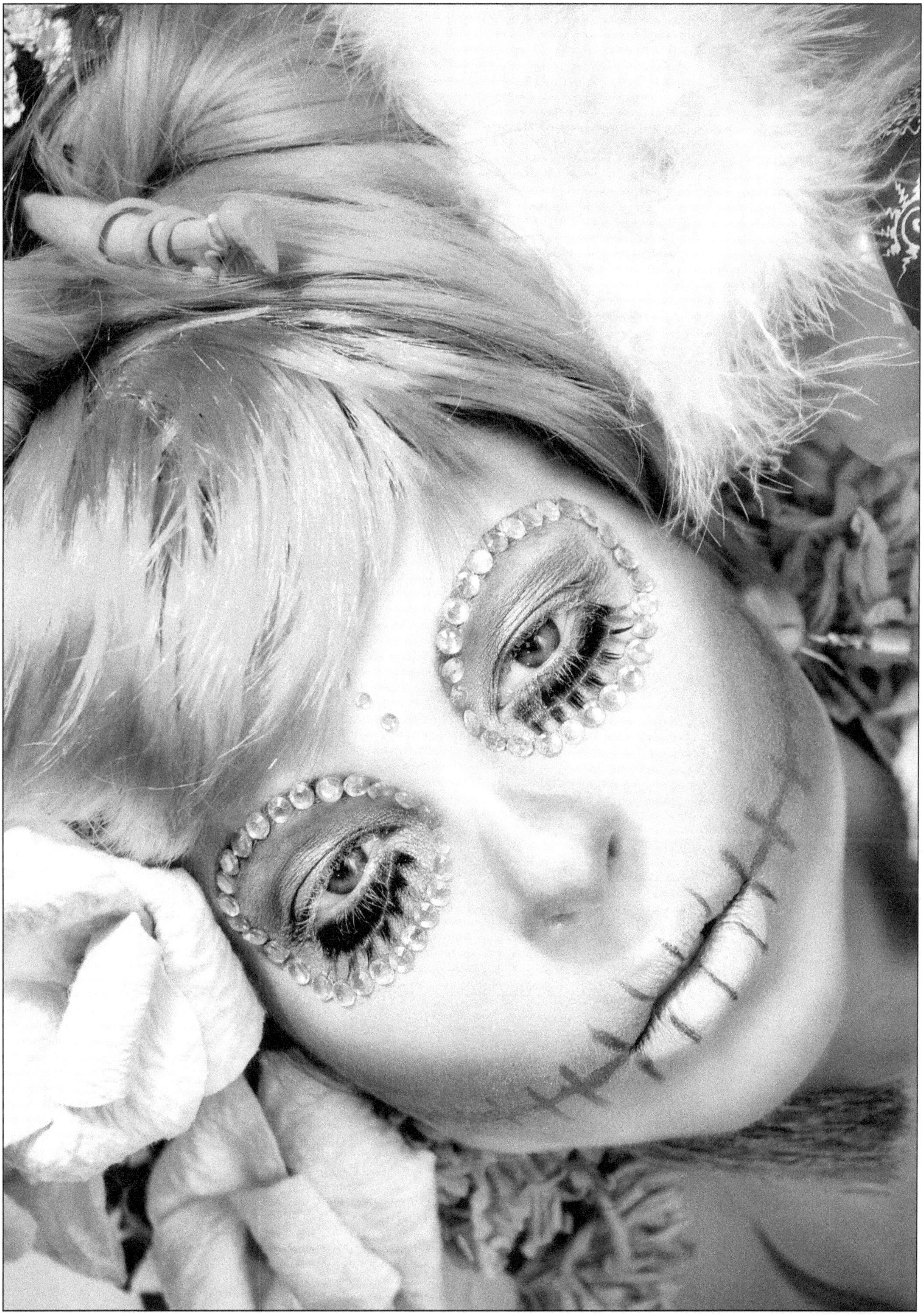

www.ingramcontent.com/pod-product-compliance
Lightning Source LLC
Chambersburg PA
CBHW080724190526
45169CB00006B/2506
* 9 7 8 1 5 3 0 5 2 7 5 0 2 *